'This is a methodologically-clear, admirably l[...] challenge; a challenge not merely to our theo[...] spiritual warfare, but to our evangelical technocratic quest for successful 'method'. Lowe argues that the floodtide of confidence in this 'method' has swept away exegetical, historical and empirical caution, and that it has unwittingly produced a synthesis uncomfortably closer to *The Testament of Solomon* (an intertestamental magical writing) and to animism than to any *biblical* understanding of demonology and spiritual warfare. In place of this questionable construction, with its quick-and-easy answers, Lowe points to the grittier, more robust example provided by James O Fraser, a CIM missionary to the Lisu in China. A great read!'

Max Turner
Vice Principal and Senior Lecturer in New Testament,
London Bible College

'So easily do many accept the new and the novel! To all who care deeply about world mission, Chuck Lowe's evaluation of strategic-level spiritual warfare is a needed clarion call; a call to reject what is built on a foundation of anecdote, speculation and animism, and to walk in the established paths of biblical truth and practice.

'Lowe has set himself up as a target for those who follow the SLSW theology. It will be interesting to see how they respond to this book.'

George Martin
Southern Baptist Theological Seminary
Louisville, Kentucky

'I am pleased to commend this careful examination of a controversial subject. The new interest in demons and the demonic, lately fanned by Peretti's novels, obliges Christians to reflect carefully on the biblical basis of all contemporary thought and practice. Not every reader will agree with the conclusions, which are sharply critical of Peter Wagner and others. But you do not have to go along with their theology to take seriously the devil and his minions.'

Nigel M. de S. Cameron
Distinguished Professor of Theology and Culture,
Trinity Evangelical Divinity School, Deerfield, Illinois

'The evangelical community at large owes Chuck Lowe a huge debt of gratitude. With his incisive, biblical analysis of strategic-level spiritual warfare, he shows clarity and sanity. He thoughtfully analyses the biblical, historical and theological tenets of our times with regard to spiritual warfare, showing them to be the re-emergence of the inter-testamental period and the medieval age. He makes a complex subject readable and concise, while remaining charitably irenic toward other Christians with whom he takes issue.

'The greatest strength of this book is the author's dogged insistence that, whatever one's approach to SLSW, one must not build doctrine on vague texts, assumptions, analogies or inferences, but on clear, solid, biblical evidence alone. I fully endorse the contents of this exceptional work.'

Richard Mayhue
Senior Vice President and Dean,
The Master's Seminary, Sun Valley, California

'The Bible makes it very clear that the forces of evil are strong, and that the followers of Jesus are engaged in an unrelenting battle against them. But little attention is given to this struggle in a good deal of modern writing, so Dr. Lowe's study of spiritual warfare is important. He is concerned with modern approaches that do not do justice to what the Bible teaches about the forces of evil. Specifically he deals with those who advocate strategic-level spiritual warfare. His book clarifies many issues, and encourages readers in their task of opposing evil.'

Leon Morris
Ridley College,
Australia

Territorial Spirits
and
World Evangelisation

A biblical, historical and missiological
critique of
Strategic-Level Spiritual Warfare

CHUCK LOWE

Mentor/OMF

ISBN 1 857 92 399 5

Published in 1998 by Christian Focus Publications, Geanies House,
Fearn, Ross-shire, IV20 1TW, Great Britain and OMF, Station Approach,
Borough Green, Sevenoaks, Kent, TN15 8BG, Great Britain.
Printed in Great Britain by J. W. Arrowsmith Limited, Bristol

CONTENTS

OMF International was founded by James Hudson Taylor in 1865 as the China Inland Mission. It now has members from 30 nations working in countries along the Asia Pacific Rim. While evangelism and church planting are the Fellowship's central thrust, it also finds placements for Christian professionals with a wide range of expertise.

Dr Lowe, a lecturer at Singapore Bible College, writes from practical missionary experience. He teaches students from the whole range of Asia's cultures and church backgrounds, and in his position he needs to maintain a clear grasp of the global trends in evangelism and prayer that come and go.

As a member of OMF International, he is concerned to see God glorified through the urgent evangelisation of East Asia's millions, and he believes wholeheartedly in the authority of Scripture and the power of prayer.

Here he examines the question of what has become known as 'Strategic Warfare Praying'. His views are not to be seen as a formal statement of Mission Policy, but the Fellowship commends this book as an encouragement to recognise the indispensable place of prayer in evangelism.

OMF English Speaking Centres

OMF
Station Approach
Borough Green
Sevenoaks
Kent TN15 8BG
UK

OMF
PO Box 849
Epping
NSW 2121
AUSTRALIA

OMF
5759 Coopers Avenue
Mississauga ONL4Z 1R9
CANADA

OMF
2 Cluny Road
Singapore 259570
REPUBLIC OF SINGAPORE

OMF
PO Box 10-159
Balmoral
Auckland 1
NEW ZEALAND

OMF
10 West Dry Creek Circle
Littleton
CO 80120-4413
USA

OMF
PO Box 3080
Pinegowrie 2123
SOUTH AFRICA

ACKNOWLEDGEMENTS

In the course of writing this book I have run up a number of substantial debts. Frugal by temperament, I prefer to postpone repayment. So I issue these IOUs.

To begin work, I needed lavish amounts of spare time. My two bosses, Mr David Pickard (General Director of the OMF International) and Rev Michael Shen (Principal of Singapore Bible College) proved generous in the extreme, and correspondingly patient.

Progress was generally facilitated (though also occasionally impeded, given my electronic ineptitude) by the generous provision of two computers, gifts respectively from Pastor David and Loo Geok Lang and from Rev Fong Yang and Constance Wong.

Sanity was retained – at least most of whatever I started with was preserved – through the provision of quiet work space. This was the gift of Rev Byron Wheaton, who moved his office into a container so that I might take over his desk. At the same time, I acknowledge that this may be the smallest sacrifice he has made in befriending me these many years.

A number of friends helpfully read and critiqued earlier versions. Among these were Rev Daniel Chua, Rev Chua Hock Guan, Pastor Peter Lim, Elder Chong Ser Choon, Rev Robert Lum, Pastor Alvin Ngo, and the title-less but never colorless Choy Wai Fann. A contingent of MDiv candidates at Singapore Bible College also suffered through a semester with this material, and deserve a long-service award (and perhaps a hazardous-duty bonus).

Finally, my long-suffering family deserves commendation for enduring my protracted preoccupation with doctrines of demons. My wife and children spent many a dreary mealtime listening to me grumble about one detail or another. Their tolerance cannot be repaid, but it should at least be acknowledged.

Now it is customary to add a little note to the effect that none of the aforementioned individuals should be held responsible for the faults in what follows. Yet, to be entirely truthful, had I not been given the time, computers, office space, sounding board, and personal support, I certainly would never have finished the project, and likely would never have started. So just as they deserve the credit, they also share the blame.

Nonetheless, I admit that none of them read the final draft before publication. So perhaps they are even now repenting of their generosity. In the words of a whimsical Scotsman, 'There is a lesson in there somewhere, if I could just put my finger on it.'

INTRODUCTION

SPIRITUAL WARFARE:
A NEW THEORY & A NEW PRACTICE

Summary: A new approach to spiritual warfare has become popular recently. While it has considerable benefits, its novelty compels careful evaluation.

A new approach to spiritual warfare is sweeping through evangelical churches and missions. Gone, its exponents tell us, are the flaccid prayer meetings of times past. No longer does prayer focus on little Jimmy's toothache. No longer do we offer token prayers for faceless missionaries on distant shores.

The enemy is after our kids, our churches, our communities, our world. This is hand-to-hand combat: graphic, impassioned, electrifying and exhilarating. Them or us, life or death, now or never. These are extraordinary times; they demand extraordinary measures.

THE GENERAL BACKGROUND

Spurred on by the best selling novels of Frank Peretti, with lurid descriptions of grotesque, sulphur-spewing demons circling small towns, threatening children and overthrowing elected governments, many Christians have awakened to the reality of spiritual warfare.[1]

Motivation to pray has increased exponentially in response to the vision of demonic hordes, locked in celestial combat with angels of light, swords clashing, wounds oozing black blood, with prayer the decisive factor determining whether the forces of good triumph over – or fall victim to – the satanic darkness.

Worried by the precipitous decline of moral values, threatened by the growing menace of New Age religions, and offended by the marginalisation of their faith, Christians are finding these to be perilous times. Satan is on the move; our world crumbles around us. Is there nothing we can do?

The New Outlook

For several decades – perhaps even a century or more – church leaders have been preoccupied with concrete measures designed to increase effectiveness in ministry: techniques such as emotive hymns, prolonged altar calls, bigger parking lots, homogeneous units, management principles, personality assessments and marketing techniques.

Now there is scant time for such mundane matters, as Christians turn to the unseen battles of darkness and light, good and evil, heaven and hell. But having awakened to the reality of the spiritual battle, many are apprehensive. How can so few win against so many? How shall mere mortals defeat demons?

Into this gap steps a bold band of prophetic leaders with an innovative strategy for winning the war. The battle plan focuses on powerful weapons of prayer, and provides training sessions to prepare mighty warriors for combat against the powers of darkness.

The conditions are desperate, and the conflict perilous. But help is at hand, and with it comes hope. We can be victorious, we are assured, even over Satan and his hordes, if we fight not in our own strength, but with newly discovered, divinely revealed, empirically verified methods.

The New Strategy
Christians have long spoken about spiritual warfare, and occasionally even practised it. But there has been little attempt to understand the principles of warfare, to systematise its procedures, or to construct a rationale sufficient to motivate diligence in practice.

Traditionally it has seemed adequate merely to affirm that our Christian lives and ministries involve a battle against spiritual forces of evil; that Satan actively opposes whatever we do for God. There has generally been little awareness of the seriousness of the battle, and little passion for actively engaging in it.

This has all changed in the last few years. 'Strategic-level spiritual warfare' (SLSW) seeks to remedy the casual, take-it-for-granted approach to spiritual warfare characteristic of traditional evangelicalism. The new warfare engages in detailed analysis of the enemy and his methods of operation, identifies the chinks in his armour, and develops a strategy to defeat him.

This new methodology has captured the popular imagination and is making considerable inroads into missionary thinking and strategy. The results are extraordinary. A new-found enthusiasm for prayer has swept many churches. Large numbers of mission teams travel on brief but costly trips into remote countries in order to challenge the spiritual forces of darkness in combative prayer. Books are written by the dozen, seminars held around the world, study groups formed, marches scheduled, all with one purpose: to disarm the spiritual powers of wickedness that impede the spread of the gospel.

THE NEED FOR EVALUATION
Proponents have high hopes. Conducted properly, SLSW promises 'unprecedented forward advances of the Kingdom of God.'[2] It purportedly offers the key to bringing ten million Japanese to Christ by AD 2000, far surpassing the meagre results of the preceding century.[3] For

its leading practitioners, this is 'one of the most important things the Spirit is saying to the churches in the 1990s.'[4] It offers missions '*the greatest power boost it has had since the time that William Carey went to India in 1793.*'[5] Yet not everyone is convinced.

The Benefits of SLSW
Because of the enthusiasm generated by such claims, many Christians and churches have embraced SLSW eagerly, without examining its actual teachings. For the first time in memory, missions strategists are affirming the existence and malevolence of demons. Prayer meetings are crowded and vibrant. Christians are lifting their eyes beyond their insular local domains, and are recovering an interest in missions. Given such positive results, it seems counter-productive to question the new teaching.

Yet these benefits may not depend on the distinctive features of SLSW. Throughout the ages the Church has affirmed the existence of demons and has performed exorcism. There have always been disciplined and devoted prayer warriors; this is no recent invention. The vast majority of missionaries have committed their lives to spreading the gospel without ever attending a single conference promoting SLSW.

None of these positive outcomes requires – or justifies – the unique teachings of SLSW. Demons exist, prayer is crucial, missions is divinely ordained; all this is true whether or not the distinctive beliefs and practices of SLSW are valid.

Whatever benefits accrue from SLSW, they come at a price. They arrive in the company of a new theology concerning demons and a new practice of spiritual warfare. It is crucial to examine both the teaching and the practice, to assess whether their benefits exceed – or are exceeded by – their cost.

Grounds for Caution
If SLSW is correct, then where the church has not spread, it is largely because missionaries did not do the job properly. So be it: embarrassment and repentance are a small price to pay for new-found evangelistic effectiveness. Proponents of SLSW are not our opponents for criticising our past methods; they are our benefactors, if their promises of spectacular success can actually be fulfilled.

Yet if SLSW is wrong, then the negative consequences are numerous and serious. It induces guilt and promotes self-doubt, inevitably albeit unintentionally. It encourages missionaries to take time away from God-given responsibilities in the vain hope of some easier or more effective, but ultimately futile, technique.

SLSW consumes enormous resources in money, time and personnel, sending people on expensive short-term prayer journeys around the world, and teaching residential personnel to engage in extraordinarily detailed mapping of entire neighbourhoods, down to the type and colour of housing on each street.[6] So, too, it may unwittingly encourage the belief that the battle for world evangelisation can be won without the arduous struggle of learning a new language, and the stress and strain of adapting to a new culture.

While raising initial hopes with promises of extraordinary results, SLSW could well end up deepening the discouragement that often accompanies years of ministry with limited response. At a time when the average duration of service for career missionaries is alarmingly low, and when the proportion of short-term volunteers is sky-rocketing, a quick key to effective ministry would be invaluable. But a false key – or the expectation of a key where there is none – could prove disastrous.

Justification for Evaluation

Passions have already been stirred over this issue. Some have committed their ministries and reputations to this new doctrine and practice. For many it has become a new test of orthodoxy and orthopraxy: a new basis for unity, and thus a grounds for division. Others are beginning to raise strenuous objections, and the first sign of disagreement has touched raw nerves.

Sometimes criticism is disparaged as reactionary traditionalism: 'The knee-jerk Christian reaction when opposing any innovation is to say, "It is not biblical".'[7] But prominent members of the charismatic, 'Third-Wave', Pentecostal and spiritual-warfare networks have been among the forefront of those objecting to the teaching.[8]

Other times the criticism is dismissed as uncharitable, theological one-up-manship, an attempt to make the critic look good by making brothers and sisters in Christ look bad.[9] Admittedly, it would be less embarrassing for evaluation to occur in private before publication rather than in public after the books are released. Yet unlike Catholicism, evangelicalism sets no requirement for pre-publication review of new ideas.

For us, unfortunately, the only court of truth is public opinion. We are democratic and entrepreneurial. In the spirit of free enterprise, anyone can propagate any belief, no matter how absurd or heretical, provided a publisher is willing to take a chance on market demand. Once promotional literature has been disseminated far and wide, it is too late to call for private discussion.[10]

Such critique does not reflect resistance to the Spirit, or a heart of unbelief toward God. Rather, it submits to Scripture's own incessant demand that all new teaching be carefully assessed, including that which purports to come from the Spirit of God (see, for example, Deut 13:1-18; 18:21-22; 1 Cor 14:29-30; 2 Cor 11:13-15; Gal 1:8; 1 Tim 4:1-6,16; 6:3-5; 6:20-21; 2 Tim 1:13-14; 2:14-19; 2:23-26; 3:14-17; 4:2-4). The same apostle who calls for love and unity (John 13:34-35; 17:20-23) engages in strenuous and public criticism of erroneous teaching which claims to come from the Spirit of God (1 John 4:1-3; 2 John 7-11; 3 John 9-10). Evaluation of SLSW – or any other new teaching – is not only justified but imperative.

Nevertheless, it must be remembered that this is an intramural debate between evangelical, mission-oriented Christians. It is not a holy war. The issue has significant theological and missiological ramifications; it should not be dismissed as a quibble about words, signifying nothing. In such circumstances, emotional detachment is neither possible nor desirable. But truth and charity should nonetheless walk hand-in-hand.

CHAPTER ONE

STRATEGIC-LEVEL SPIRITUAL WARFARE:
A NEW TYPE OF DEMON and
A NEW WAY OF FIGHTING

Summary: 'Territorial spirits' are purportedly a class of powerful demons that rule over jurisdictions of various types and sizes. 'Warfare prayer' involves naming and rebuking the spirits, in order to reach the world for Christ. The terminology needs some refinement, and the teaching needs careful evaluation.

Any critique is obliged, in large measure, to follow the agenda set by the theory which it evaluates. Consequently, this book does not offer a systematic treatment of biblical teaching concerning Satan, demons, exorcism or even spiritual warfare.[11] It presupposes the existence of demons, the legitimacy of exorcism (at least, of some exorcisms), and the need for spiritual warfare of some sort. These are not the issues at hand. Instead, the critique centres on the distinctives of SLSW.

WHAT IS STRATEGIC-LEVEL SPIRITUAL WARFARE?

On the surface, this is a simple question to answer. Strategic-level spiritual warfare consists of two major components: the theory of 'strategic-level spirits' and the practice of 'spiritual warfare'. The first describes a newly postulated kind of demon, and the latter refers to a new strategy designed specifically to defeat them. More commonly the former are called 'territorial spirits', and the latter is known as 'warfare prayer'. So far, however, this answer is not especially illuminating. All it does is to introduce labels. The rest of this chapter fleshes out that verbal skeleton.

What Are Territorial Spirits?

Back in the hoary days of my youth, a favourite diversion for hikers and campers was 'snipe-hunting'. First-timers would be invited to go out on a hunt late some night. The invitation would inevitably be met with the query: What is a snipe? Some vague but confident answer would lure the victim into the ruse. A long hike into the woods late at night would end with the hapless victim out in the middle of nowhere without a flashlight or a ride back to the campsite.

Snipe hunts are rather fun on hiking trips, and if you are not the victim. But they do not make for sound theological inquiry. Before we go looking for evidence that territorial spirits actually exist, it makes a fair bit of sense to figure out what exactly they look like.

There are essentially two approaches to describing territorial spirits. The first compares and contrasts them with other types of demons. The second focuses on the meaning of 'territorial'. The two methods are not mutually exclusive, so both will be explored here. Unfortunately, neither method yields clear or consistent results.

Are There Three Classes of Demons?

According to leading advocate Peter Wagner, demons fall into three basic categories: ground-level, occult-level and strategic-level.[12]

Ground-level spirits are the sort that possess people and must be exorcised. Occult-level spirits empower magicians, witches, warlocks and shaman. Strategic-level spirits (otherwise known as cosmic-level, or territorial, spirits) are the most powerful of the three categories. Their function is to rule over specific domains, preventing the people that reside there from coming to faith. So the proposed differences between the three categories involve both power and function: strategic-level spirits are the highest ranking class of demons and they are territorial in jurisdiction.[13]

While this seems clear enough in theory, in practice it is difficult to find examples of such spirits without blurring the distinctions. Thus, in the search for historical precedent, Wagner quotes a number of early Church Fathers, including Justin, Irenaeus, Tertullian and Cyprian.[14] But the Fathers merely affirm the reality of demon possession and the effectiveness of exorcism. These should be ground-level, not strategic-level, spirits.

The blurring of distinctions also occurs in the citation of secondary sources. Susan Garrett's work on Luke-Acts is often invoked to support the existence of territorial spirits.[15] But as her subtitle indicates, she is interested exclusively in the connection between magic and demons: *The Demise of the Devil: Magic and the Demonic in Luke's Writings*. According to the proposed taxonomy, these are occult-level spirits.

Similarly, in his survey of historical evidence, Wagner makes frequent and extensive appeal to Ramsay MacMullen's work, which attributes the rapid growth of the church between AD 100-400 in part to its mastery of the spirit world.[16] In actual fact, however, all of MacMullen's examples refer to ground-level or occult-level spirits (though he neither uses these terms nor differentiates these categories).

The ambiguity also arises in the treatment of the biblical texts. Three times in Acts the apostles confront sorcery: Simon the magician (8:9-24), Elymas the sorcerer (13:6-12), and the clairvoyant slave girl of Philippi (16:16-18). Given their function, these should be occult-level spirits. Each, however, is identified as strategic-level.[17]

The rationale for the identification is instructive. Concerning the confrontation between the apostle Paul and Elymas the magician in Acts 13, Wagner comments:

> Although we are dealing with a person, Bar-Jesus (ground level), and although that person is an occult practitioner (occult level), I believe *the magnitude of the event* places it, in the invisible world, on the strategic level.[18]

If so, then the distinctive characteristic of strategic-level spirits is not function but rank.

The confrontation between the apostle Peter and Simon the magician in Acts confirms this modification,[19] as does the exorcism of the divination spirit from the slave girl in Philippi (Acts 16).[20] In justifying his interpretation of the latter, Wagner explains that the distinction between the three classes depends on 'the rank of the spirit.'[21]

In the end, however, even this modified distinction does not work consistently. Thus, when confronted with a purportedly strategic-level spirit in Ephesus (Acts 19:1-20), Paul engages only in ground-level and occult-level spiritual warfare.[22] Wagner comments:

> Better than any other passage of Scripture, Acts 19 shows us clearly how the world of darkness is interconnected, overriding the somewhat artificial lines some of us have drawn separating ground-level, occult-level and strategic-level spiritual warfare.[23]

In the final analysis, Wagner acknowledges, the Bible does not provide a single definite example of a specifically strategic-level spirit.[24]

If the lines are 'somewhat artificial',[25] why draw them at all? If the functional differences between demon classes are inconsequential or indeterminate, why does function feature prominently in their description? If there is not a single definite strategic-level spirit in Scripture, why are so many examples cited from the Bible? Since the differentiation of spirits into three classes is unproductive and inconsistent, it is best abandoned.

What Is the Meaning of 'Territorial'?

The second method for defining strategic-level spirits focuses on their central characteristic: they are purportedly 'territorial'. Unfortunately, the meaning of this description – and thus the function of the class – is ambiguous.

At first blush, the term seems self-explanatory: these are demons which rule over specified geographical regions. They are 'geographically located', exercise authority within 'assigned areas', and have 'geographical limits for their power.'[26] Thus, the back cover of the British edition of an early book edited by Wagner specifically asks: *Territorial Spirits: Are Evil Spirits Assigned to Geographical Regions?*[27] Clearly the intended answer is affirmative. Thus, for example, the 'prince of Persia' (Dan 10:13, 20) is taken to be 'an evil spiritual being ruling over an area with explicitly proscribed [sic] boundaries.'[28]

Strategic-level spirits of various ranks rule over geographical regions of corresponding size, including towns, cities and nations.[29] One demon is purportedly restricted to Costa Rica, and its victim gains relief by travelling to the United States.[30] Another exercises its malignant influence only within the confines of a Navajo reservation, and has no power outside those boundaries.[31] Those who serve such spirits are reluctant to leave their villages for fear of being unprotected; those who do leave must embrace the gods of their new village.[32]

Related terms and practices reflect a similar geographical focus. A 'seat of Satan' is 'a geographical location that is highly oppressed and demonically controlled by a certain dark principality.'[33] Spiritual mapping catalogues spirits by geographical regions.[34] Mapping can be done on 'virtually any geographical area.'[35] Various types of perambulatory prayer counteract these spirits by praying throughout neighbourhoods ('prayerwalks'), cities ('praise marches'), regions ('prayer expeditions') or nations ('prayer journeys').[36]

But other times geographical distinctions are superseded by some other characteristic. For instance, 'rule #1' for 'taking a city' is to 'select a manageable geographical area.'[37] Yet by 'rule #6', it turns out that spirits are assigned not only to geographical regions but also to social, cultural, ethnic, or 'other networks of humans.'[38]

On closer examination it turns out that territorial demons are purportedly assigned not only to geographical regions, but also to geopolitical institutions, such as nations or states;[39] to topographical features, such as valleys, mountains or rivers;[40] to ecological features, such as trees, streams and rocks;[41] or to smaller physical objects, such as houses, temples or idols.[42]

Given this ambiguity, another term would be preferable. 'Territorial' is too suggestive of geographical limits; in the end, it is used in so many different senses that it becomes irretrievably vague. What is needed is a designation which is narrow enough to capture the distinctive role of these spirits yet broad enough to incorporate the variety of jurisdictions attributed to them. But before a more suitable designation can be selected, one final ambiguity must be raised.

Are the Spirits Custodial or Residential?

Generally strategic-level spirits are portrayed as custodial. They 'dominate' an area,[43] or 'control' a town.[44] They exercise 'supervision',[45] serve as 'rulers',[46] or have 'custody over' their realm.[47] All of these terms share the concept of custodianship or sovereignty.

Sometimes, however, the concept of demons ruling over territories also develops into – or is confused with – the idea of spirits residing in geographical regions.[48]

This idea is implicit in the common justification for such spirits. Satan, as a created being, is not omnipresent. So if he is to blind the world's peoples, he requires the assistance of innumerable strategic-level spirits.[49] By this logic demonic powers can affect a place only while residing there.

Thus, demons may 'occupy' geographical regions,[50] 'attach' themselves to buildings and idols,[51] or indwell trees or mountains.[52] In such cases, they are perceived to be 'geographically located'.[53]

Summary

The multiple ambiguities come to a head in a commonly quoted explanation:

> Satan delegates *high ranking* members of the hierarchy of evil spirits to *control* nations, regions, cities, tribes, people groups, neighbourhoods and other significant *social networks* of human beings throughout the world. Their major assignment is to prevent God from being glorified in their *territory*, which they do through directing the activity of lower ranking demons.
>
> It can immediately be seen that this hypothesis will stand or fall on the issue of whether spirits or demonic beings can legitimately be perceived as *occupying territories*.[54]

Is the defining characteristic of these spirits their high rank, their controlling function, or a combination of the two? Is their jurisdiction delimited by geography, political bureaucracy, ethnicity, social structure, or some other feature? Do they merely govern territories, or do they also occupy them? Due to these ambiguities, it does not follow that 'this hypothesis will stand or fall on the issue of whether spirits or demonic beings can legitimately be perceived as *occupying territories*'.

Some ambiguities persist in the most recent book on this topic. On one page it seems 'territorial' is returning to the narrower definition of geographically specificity:

> From time to time I have used the term 'territorial spirits.' This is not to imply that every demon is confined to a limited geographical arena, but it is to imply that some, perhaps many, might well be.[55]

This explanation reflects two changes. For one, diffidence replaces certainty. For the other, 'territorial' now implies 'a limited geographical arena', and territorial spirits are contrasted with non-territorial types.

Two pages later, two characteristics appear to differentiate territorial spirits, geographical specificity and higher rank:

> Wherever human beings group themselves together, such as *in neighbourhoods, in cities, in regions or in nations*, it could be expected that *higher-ranking spirits*, who have many others under their command, would be assigned. They are the ones we sometimes refer to as 'territorial spirits.' Where people develop a group affinity such as religious allegiance or vocation or some voluntary associations, however, the spirits over them might not be so *confined to a geographical territory*. For example, I would not be surprised if certain principalities were assigned to industries such as the meat-packing industry or the gold-mining industry or the automobile industry and so on.[56]

This quote appears to confirm that 'territorial' is returning to a narrower geographically-based definition, and excludes other sorts of specialisation. At the same time, it also explicitly reintroduces a second element, demonic hierarchies. A familiar third characteristic seems also to be implied: that these demons not merely exercise authority over a specified region, but reside within, and are restricted to, that location.

This is not pointless quibbling over terminology. These distinctions are crucial for those who directly confront the spirit world, whether in worship, in spiritual warfare, or in theological analysis.

If the spirits are geographical, then migrants must leave their old gods behind, and embrace new ones. If the spirits are ethnic, then their worshippers may carry them along to new lands. If spirits are geopolitical, then nations vanquished in war must embrace the gods of their conquerors; but if they are geographical, then it is the invaders who must change gods. Corresponding implications follow, depending on whether the spirits are domestic, occupational, ecological, and so forth.

Similarly, if spirits are geographical, then missionaries must engage in concentrated spiritual warfare whenever they enter a new region (however narrowly or widely that may be defined). On the other hand, if the spirits are topographical or ecological, then spiritual warfare is necessary only in the vicinity of religiously significant mountains, rivers, stones or trees. If spirits are ethnic, then spiritual warfare is particularly mandated when penetrating a new tribe or people-group, but may not be necessary when beginning a new outreach in a new area to other members of an evangelised people-group.

If multifarious demonic specialisation is in view, then the current widespread preoccupation with geographical demons is a dangerously flawed strategy. It serves no useful function to guard against one type of spirit while allowing all others free rein. There is an urgent need to devise specialised techniques for freeing the world from the demons over each religion, each vocation, each voluntary association, and so forth. What good would it do to free people from the demons which rule their towns, without freeing them from the demons that rule their occupations or leisure activities?

These distinctions are also crucial if the discussion is to make head-way. The dialogue will not be productive without initial agreement concerning the topic of discussion and the meaning of terms.

The characteristics of the spirits also affect the kind of evidence needed to substantiate their existence. If the spirits are meant to be geographically specific, then the only line of useful evidence would be geographical. Citing evidence of topographical, ethnic, geopolitical, functional or ecological spirits would be irrelevant, if not counter-productive.

If, as one suspects, the core proposition is simply that demons rule over the world and its affairs, then discussion can usefully centre on this issue. Demon hierarchies, taxonomies, territories, and residences are secondary questions, best left aside for the moment.

If this is primarily what is meant, though, the coining of a new label obscures the fact that the concept is centuries old. Early Church Fathers spoke of such spirits, as did the Protestant Reformers (see chapter 6). Moreover, the coining of a misleading designation creates considerable confusion.

For historical continuity and for clarity, then, it is advisable to return to the traditional label, 'tutelary spirits', or to the simpler, 'guardian spirits' or 'ruling spirits'. Where it is necessary to distinguish different sorts of jurisdiction, more precise labels are necessary, such as 'geographical', 'geopolitical', 'ethnic', 'topographical', 'ecological', 'domestic', 'ancestral', 'cultic', 'occupational', or 'functional' spirits.

What is Warfare Prayer?

Traditional 'spiritual warfare' seems more akin to a trip to the local fast-food restaurant than to the battlefield. Armed with a long list of assorted items desired on the occasion, we pull in to the drive-up window, and call out the preferred items, receive our order and drive off again, the quicker the better.

Or at least we hope that it will work that smoothly. More commonly it would seem that the staff is under training. We get some items we did not want, and fail to receive others which were high on our agenda. But never mind. Something is better than nothing, and we can take another drive by sometime next week in the hopes of obtaining more. So long as our expectations are not too high, the service is tolerable. Above all else, it offers convenience and comfort: no exertion, no discipline, no delay.

The Central Characteristic

Bored by such lethargy and frustrated with such mediocrity, advocates of SLSW are declaring war, not only on evil spirits, but also on the standard practice of spiritual warfare. In its place they offer 'warfare prayer'.

Conceivably either the theory of territorial spirits or the practice of warfare prayer could be endorsed without implying the other. In actual fact, however, they keep close company. Indeed, the standard terminology explicitly combines the two: 'strategic-level spiritual warfare'. This is a new sort of spiritual warfare, designed specifically to respond to a new (or newly discovered) sort of spirit.

Warfare prayer has one overriding characteristic: aggression. This is meant in two senses: Christians are to go on the offensive, and, in a manner of speaking, they are entitled to be offensive. Passivity is out; pugnacity is in.[57]

The Specific Practices

Warfare prayer has essentially two steps. The first is to seek the name of the ruling spirit and to identify its territory. The proper name of the demon is preferable; if this proves too difficult to obtain, a functional name (for example, 'demon of lying') is better than nothing.[58] Identifying the territory ensures that the proper demon is selected, and establishes the boundaries for ministry once the demon is bound.

Possession of this information renders the spirits more vulnerable to attack.[59] The second step of using a demon's name in direct rebuke conveys power over it. Once this is done, evangelism purportedly proceeds with far greater effectiveness.[60]

An occasional concession acknowledges that revival has come in the past without this technique. Even then, greater results could have been achieved with it.[61] But in present times SLSW is more urgent than ever before, because as the end of the world approaches, demonic opposition has become 'unique in both type and magnitude. Commonplace methods of discerning and responding to these challenges will no longer do.'[62]

At times the expectation is moderate: those who practice SLSW are 'able to free the cities and nations of the world from the powers of darkness in order to ready them for spiritual harvest.... Our prayers will release regions from the influence of these powers for a season while we go in and harvest.'[63]

At other times the promise is dramatic: 'The prayer of a human being can alter history by releasing legions of angels into the earth.'[64] SLSW helped to bring down the Berlin Wall, open Albania to the gospel, depose Manuel Noriega, lower the crime rate in Los Angeles during the 1984 Olympics, revive the economy in Argentina, and break the power of the demons over Japan.[65]

But at all times, SLSW is portrayed as the key to effective evangelisation. 'Through warfare prayer, we can free unsaved souls and take them "from darkness to light, and from the power of Satan to God".'[66] Warfare prayer 'helps bring about effective evangelism,'[67] and can increase receptivity to the gospel 'virtually overnight.'[68]

Summary

Terminology is again a problem. Some critics object to the label 'warfare prayer': this is aggressive challenge, directed against the demons; prayer is meant to be supplication, addressed to God.

There is some legitimacy to this protest. One could hope for a more appropriate designation, one more consistent with the usual concept of prayer. Yet since there is no commonly accepted alternative, it seems necessary to use 'warfare prayer', alternatively with 'binding' or 'cursing' the spirits.

In any event, granting that the terminology is less than ideal, the crucial question concerns the legitimacy of the procedure. Is there precedent for naming the ruling spirits? Does using the name in direct command provide greater power over the spirits? Does this procedure fulfil its claim to unprecedented effectiveness in evangelism and missions?

EVALUATING STRATEGIC-LEVEL WARFARE

The way a question is phrased can prejudice the answer. So it is crucial to identify the specific issues under debate, and to define them in such a way as to be acceptable to all parties.

In a recent contribution to the discussion, Wagner begins with a helpful clarification of what is not at issue: 'The controversy that has developed in the 1990s should not be seen as questioning whether Christians should or should not engage in spiritual warfare.'[69] This is a crucial point. All parties to this discussion agree that Satan is a powerful and malicious opponent. All affirm that Christians are to engage in spiritual warfare.

What, then, is the focus of the controversy? For Wagner, the decisive question is, 'How much power did Jesus give His disciples?'[70] He elaborates:

> Some critics of strategic-level spiritual warfare argue that Jesus set boundaries to the power He offered the disciples through the Holy Spirit. They suggest that we may not have authority over all the powers of darkness, just over the lower-level demons that may be demonising human beings. Therefore we should stay away from strategic-level spiritual warfare, lest we overstep our legitimate authority. [71]

If the question is put in this way, the answer is obvious:

> Jesus said, 'Behold, I give you the authority to trample on serpents and scorpions, *and over all the power of the enemy* [Luke 10:19].... The question then becomes, did Jesus mean 'all' when He made this particular promise? I think He did.[72]

Thus Luke 10:19 features prominently in Wagner's argument, appearing at least six times in the one volume.[73]

This statement of the issue is ironic. Sandwiched between these two preceding quotes, Wagner acknowledges:

It is true, as the critics point out, that the examples we have in the Gospels of the ministry of Jesus' disciples deal by and large with what is called ground-level spiritual warfare.[74]

Furthermore, though the book represents his best efforts to amass support for the theory,[75] he acknowledges that there is not a single indisputable instance of strategic-level spiritual warfare in the New Testament. He admits that each of the examples he cites could be interpreted as something other than SLSW.[76] The most he claims to offer is '*evidence*' not '*proof.*'[77]

The fundamental issue, then, has little to do with limits on the authority of Christians. Rather, it centres on the legitimacy of the proposed taxonomy and the appropriateness of the recommended strategy.

To support SLSW, it is not sufficient to find biblical texts or empirical data confirming the existence of demons or enjoining spiritual warfare. Both are undeniably taught in Scripture and widely practised in the church. Instead, support must be directed toward the distinctive characteristics of SLSW. Consequently this critique focuses on the theory of territorial spirits and the practice of warfare prayer.

The Issues

Is there a special class of ruling spirits, distinct from those types of demons which possess people or which empower magicians? Do these ruling spirits subdivide the world into a bureaucratic hierarchy? If so, how are their various jurisdictions differentiated: are the boundaries geographical, socio-political, ethnic, ecological, or what?

How are these demons overcome? Should we identify their names and functions, and use these names in confrontation and imprecation? Will this produce greater results than some more traditional, less aggressive form of spiritual warfare?

A number of other theories and practices are commonly linked with SLSW. 'Spiritual mapping' collates and plots the information concerning territorial spirits and their 'strongholds' for distribution and wider prayer.[78] 'Identificational repentance' seeks to deprive the spirits of a foothold in the culture or region by removing the sin and guilt which purportedly enable them to gain entry.[79] Perambulatory prayer on site (such as 'prayer walks', 'prayer marches', 'prayer expeditions', and 'prayer journeys') allegedly increases the effectiveness of the prayer.[80]

Among some practitioners these additional features are core activities.[81] But at least theoretically, SLSW is coherent without them. Consequently, the analysis which follows focuses on the core theory and practice, and refers to these other features only in passing and where especially relevant.

The Evidence

The lines of evidence cited in promotion of SLSW divide into two broad categories: biblical and extra-biblical.

The role of the biblical evidence is ambiguous. Some proponents concede that there is no biblical support for SLSW, but insist that there need not be, so long as the teaching is not anti-biblical.[82] Others insist that there both must be and is biblical support for both the theory and practice.[83] Does the Bible support SLSW? If not, may we still practise it? A survey of relevant Scriptural texts answers both questions.

The paucity of biblical evidence requires some justification. Ready at hand is the slogan, 'God is doing something new!' But is SLSW entirely new? If not, what sort of reception have similar teachings received in the past? An overview of intertestamental literature and Church history provides considerable guidance for present practice.

Evangelicalism has previously not realised the need for aggressive spiritual warfare purportedly because of undue influence from Enlightenment rationalism. We need a new paradigm, it is claimed; one which, like animism, takes more cognisance of the spirit-world. This raises two questions: Does animism affirm the existence of territorial spirits? If so, is its worldview compatible with biblical Christianity? While it is impossible to make blanket statements about the many versions of animism, a survey of several forms sheds light on this line of argument.

Undoubtedly the bulk of the argument for SLSW derives from empirical data. The literature abounds with anecdotes of notable success in ministry following the practice of SLSW. These accounts bear closer scrutiny, both on their own merits and in the light of social-science models of religious change.

The argument for SLSW depends in large measure on a false dichotomy: since the typical evangelical neglect of spiritual warfare is defective, SLSW should be embraced. There is at least one more alternative: recovery of traditional evangelical spiritual warfare. Since this historical model is less familiar, the final chapter reviews one example from earlier in this century.

Finally, lest critics of SLSW grow too harsh, the conclusion draws out two continuities between SLSW and recent evangelical trends, similarities which should prompt re-evaluation of many of our practices.

CHAPTER TWO

RULING SPIRITS:
WHAT THEY ARE AND WHAT THEY DO

Summary: The Bible does not portray demons as geographically specific. Tutelary spirits do appear on occasion, but only to make the point that opposition to the people of God is motivated by Satan. The Bible provides little additional information about demon taxonomy.

The Bible differs from systematic theology textbooks in at least two ways. First, its teachings are generally not organised topically. Instead, to answer a single question it is often necessary to range over the entire length of Scripture rather than restricting the search to a single passage. Secondly, on some issues of great interest to us, the biblical teaching is allusive and elusive. Whether it be because the biblical authors were disinterested, or the divine author considered it unimportant, many topics receive only cursory attention. The concept of ruling spirits is one such topic.

RULING SPIRITS IN THE OLD TESTAMENT

There are probably sufficient references to ruling spirits within the Old Testament to affirm their existence, but the teaching is neither explicit nor extensive.

Ruling Spirits in Deuteronomy?

The paucity of relevant data in the Old Testament forces proponents to rely heavily on a dubious reading of an uncertain text. Described as 'one of the key texts' for this theory,[84] Deuteronomy 32:8-9 reads:

> When the Most High gave the nations their inheritance,
>   when he divided all mankind,
> he set up boundaries for the peoples
>   according to the numbers of the sons of Israel.
> For the LORD's portion is his people,
>   Jacob his allotted inheritance.

The basic idea is that God divided all the nations and their territories: he kept Israel for himself, and parcelled out the other nations to the 'sons of Israel' (whatever that phrase means).

But perhaps 'sons of Israel' was not the original reading of the text. The NIV includes a footnote: the earlier manuscripts discovered amongst the Dead Sea Scrolls of Qumran read 'sons of God'. Another alternative comes from the Septuagint (an early Greek translation), which reads 'angels of God'. If the Septuagint version is original, then this verse means that God has appointed angels to serve as guardians over the nations, while he looks after Israel.

This is a lot of 'ifs', and at best this passage affirms the existence of ruling *angels*, not demons. For both reasons it cannot bear a lot of weight. But at least it raises the possibility that guardian spirits exist, though it is not clear whether these are all angels, all demons, or some of each. Nor is it clear whether their jurisdiction is geographical, geopolitical or ethnic.

Ruling Spirits in Psalms?

Another possibly relevant text is Psalm 82:1-2, which reads:

> God presides in the great assembly;
>   he gives judgement among the 'gods':
> 'How long will you defend the unjust
>   and show partiality to the wicked?'

Scholars are not agreed on the identity of these 'gods': perhaps they are human judges over the nation (cf. John 10:34); perhaps the reference is to pagan deities; or perhaps they are angelic powers behind the national rulers, that is, ruling spirits. If the last, then their corruption suggests a demonic, rather than an angelic, orientation:

> "I said, 'You are "gods";
>   you are all sons of the Most High.'
> But you will die like mere men;
>   you will fall like every other ruler." (82:6-7)

But this is again all rather tentative.

Ruling Spirits in Isaiah?

Similarly, Isaiah 24:21-22 may, or may not, affirm the existence of ruling demons:

> In that day the LORD will punish
>   the powers in the heavens above
>   and the kings on the earth below.
> They will be herded together
>   like prisoners bound in a dungeon;
> they will be shut up in prison
>   and be punished after many days.

The punishment threatened against 'the powers' implies that they are demonic. The parallel between the powers of heaven and the kings on earth could suggest that they are linked; that is, that these demons work through the kings and serve as guardians over the nations. Again, though, all this is possible but not definite, and inferential rather than explicit. It is just as likely that Isaiah refers *en bloc* to the rulers of heaven and earth, without intending any correspondence between specific spirit powers in the heavens and individual rulers on earth.[85]

Ruling Spirits in Ezekiel?

The same could be said of Ezekiel 28:12-19. The word of the Lord to the king of Tyre is:

> You were anointed as a guardian cherub,
>   for so I ordained you. . . .
> Through your widespread trade
>   you were filled with violence,
>   and you sinned.
> So I drove you in disgrace from the mount of God,
>   and I expelled you, O guardian cherub. (28:14,16)

'Cherub' is possibly a reference to a patron deity represented by and working through the human ruler of Tyre. If so, then this deity is portrayed as a demonic spirit: the guardian angel over Tyre fell into sin and was expelled from the presence of God.

But while ancient Tyre did claim the patronage of a deity called 'Melkart' ('king of the city'), in this passage the king is probably human. At least, the designation 'king' appears more than ten more times in Ezekiel, always for human rulers (for example, 17:12; 19:9; 21:19; 24:2; 29:2; 30:21; 31:2). Here the king engages in international trade and commerce, a curious occupation for a demonic spirit. Moreover, the previous message to this ruler of Tyre was:

> In the pride of your heart
>   you say, "I am a god". . . .
> But you are a man and not a god,
>   though you think you are as wise as a god. (28:2)

In the end, the symbolism of this text remains obscure to the modern interpreter. Perhaps behind the king lurks a ruling demon. Perhaps the imagery alludes to a pagan notion of divine kingship. Perhaps the king is a symbol for the city-state, proclaiming its wealth and claiming omnipotence.

All these interpretations and more have advocates, a clear sign of irremediable ambiguity.

Ruling Spirits in Daniel?

The most commonly cited Old Testament proof-text is Daniel 10:13, 20. Daniel has a dream and prays for God to reveal its interpretation. After twenty-one days an angel comes to explain both the dream and the reason for the delay:

> 'The prince of the Persian kingdom resisted me twenty-one days. Then Michael, one of the chief princes, came to help me, because I was detained there with the king of Persia.... Soon I will return to fight against the prince of Persia, and when I go, the prince of Greece will come.... No-one supports me against them except Michael, your prince.' (10:13,20-21)

Given that the archangel Michael is a 'prince' and guardian of Israel, it is reasonable to infer that the opposing 'princes' are demonic guardians over Persia and Greece. At least that is how they were understood in later Judaism and early Christianity.[86]

From this text proponents of SLSW infer the existence of an entire hierarchy of demons ruling over territories of various sizes. The first step is to infer geographical boundaries for the spirit 'princes' of Persia and Greece: 'Here we have a well-defined case of an evil spiritual being ruling over an area with explicitly defined boundaries.'[87] The next step is to assume the existence of similar ruling demons throughout the world: 'It seems safe to assume that just as there was a "prince of Persia" ..., so there are "princes" in charge of other geographical areas.'[88] The third and final step is to argue by analogy that the existence of national spirits implies the existence of lower-ranking spirits over smaller regions. Dawson concludes: 'Since Israel is a forerunner used to demonstrate God's truth to all the earth, it follows that all nations, cities and subcultures have guardian angels assigned to them.'[89]

This argument infers a lot out of a little. From demonic rulers over two nations, to demonic rulers over all nations, to demonic rulers over smaller units within each nation. Warner is right to call this hypothesis an assumption; actually it is an assumption built on an analogy and leading to an inference. Where evidence exists, assumption and inference are unnecessary.

On closer look, the foundational inference proves untenable. The 'princes' of Persia and Greece did not rule over areas 'with explicitly defined boundaries'. It is natural – but clearly erroneous – to assume that these spirits ruled over the regions of Persia and Greece, respectively.

The subsequent chapters in Daniel indicate that Persia and Greece were not fixed geographical regions, nor were they co-operative world powers. Instead, they were successive and rival empires, competitors for world dominion (Dan 11:2-35). Within the time frame of the book of Daniel, the Babylonians conquered Judah (597-582 BC; see Dan 1–5), but were soon supplanted by the Persians (538-531 BC; see Dan 6–10). Subsequently the Greek empire conquered the Persians (4th century BC; Dan 11:2), before splitting into four rival kingdoms (Dan 11:4-45).

The historical realities pose two problems for the theory of territorial spirits. Firstly, the princes of Daniel 10 rule not over nations or over fixed geographical regions, but over imperialistic empires whose boundaries expand and contract. In fact, the territories ruled by Persia and Greece were virtually coterminous, as one empire fell to the next. So the respective princes may be tutelary powers, but if so, then they are expansionistic – not geographical – spirits. Thus, Wagner concludes: 'This story leaves little doubt that *territorial* spirits greatly influence human life in all its *sociopolitical* aspects.'[90] If their effect is sociopolitical, rather than geographical, 'sociopolitical' spirits would be a clearer designation.

But this leads to the second problem. If the princes are tutelary spirits, then as one empire goes to war against another, the respective spirits fight each other. As Collins observes, 'A battle between two earthly powers is a reflection of a battle between their respective gods.'[91] This would involve civil war in the kingdom of darkness, which is clearly problematic in view of Jesus' teaching on the issue (see Matt 12:25; Luke 11:18). So if the angelic princes are understood in the sense preferred by the proponents of SLSW, SLSW is undermined.

In any event, Daniel is not interested in the structure of demonic hierarchies. He is concerned with the fate of Israel, oppressed by world powers. His point is merely that any empire which attacks Israel is opposing God and serving Satan. In that respect these powers are demonic. More than this he does not say. Nor can we.

Ruling Spirits Among the Nations?
The final line of Old Testament evidence comes not from the positive affirmations of the text, but from its descriptions of ancient Canaanite beliefs. Wagner comments:

Throughout the Old Testament, it is evident that the peoples of that day – unfortunately including Israel at certain times – regarded gods, deities, spirits or angelic powers of various kinds as having territorial jurisdiction.[92]

The logic is that if the Canaanite gods are actually demons, then the belief in territorial deities provides evidence of territorial spirits.

Before considering the specific biblical accounts, it is necessary to clarify a fundamental distinction: the difference between phenomenology (the way things are experienced) and ontology (the way things are).[93] A common example may clarify the difference. We experience the world as geocentric: the sun rises in the east, and sets in the west; it is the sun, not the earth which seems to move. That is, of course, the reason why the geocentric model prevailed in astronomy for millennia. But the geocentric model was eventually overturned for the heliocentric model. Phenomenologically, the earth seems to be the centre of the universe; ontologically, the sun is.

Unfortunately, proponents of SLSW commonly conflate phenomenology with ontology. Thus, for example, in the preceding quote, Wagner addresses phenomenology: the ancients '*regarded* gods ... as having territorial jurisdiction.'[94] But within the same paragraph he slides into ontology: 'Many of these [idols and worship sites] *had become* the literal dwelling place of demonic spirits.'[95] This begs the question: does the Old Testament merely depict – or does it actually endorse – the perception of territoriality? Does it describe people who thought this way (phenomenology) or does it affrm the legitimacy of such beliefs (ontology)? The latter must be demonstrated; it cannot simply be assumed.[96]

Turning to the actual biblical accounts, it happens that much of the data is misconstrued. Cultic high places, for example, are interpreted as 'the literal dwelling place of demonic spirits.'[97] But the Old Testament consistently describes these as 'places ... where the nations worship ... their gods' (Deut 12:2-3; cf. 2 Kgs 17:11; 23:5; 2 Chr 28:25). By my count there are eighty-six references to 'high places' in the Old Testament, yet not one states or implies that the gods are actually located at the site or restricted to it, only that they are worshiped there.

Other evidence is adduced from narratives. Ahaz, for example, 'burned sacrifices ... following the detestable ways of the nations that the LORD had driven out before the Israelites' (2 Chr 28:3). It is speculated that Ahaz worships these Canaanite gods because he assumes that they retain jurisdiction over the land even after Israel expels the Canaanites.[98]

But a closer look at the text refutes this explanation and highlights other motivations for the idolatry. Ahaz was remarkably eclectic in his worship: 'He offered sacrifices and burned incense at the high places, on the hilltops and under every spreading tree' (2 Chr 28:4). The only motivation the text ever explicitly ascribes to him is pragmatism: 'He offered sacrifices to the gods of Damascus, who had defeated him; for he thought, "Since the gods of the kings of Aram have helped them, I will sacrifice to them so that they will help me"' (2 Chr 28:23). Pragmatism, not belief in territoriality, was his justification. And his appeal was directed not to the gods of his own land, but to the gods of surrounding nations. Such prayer presupposes that the gods are not territorial, but are willing to help anyone who serves them!

While examples could be multiplied, a last one must suffice. Ben-Hadad, king of Aram, invades Samaria, but is soundly defeated (1 Kgs 20:1-21). His officials attribute the Israelite victory to topographical jurisdiction: 'Their gods are gods of the hills. That is why they were too strong for us. But if we fight them on the plains, surely we will be stronger than they' (1 Kgs 20:23). Emboldened by the advice, Ben-Hadad rebuilds his army and attacks a year later, only to be defeated again. Wagner concludes:

> This shows that the Syrians [Arameans] perceived ruling spirits to have, if *not territoriality*, at least *topographical* jurisdiction. Nothing in the passage or elsewhere in the Old Testament contradicts their perception of *territorial* spirits ruling areas. The assumption is that they were correct. Their big error was that they wrongly considered Jehovah God as just another territorial spirit.[99]

Several comments are in order.

First, Wagner is right to note that this account endorses topographical, rather than territorial, jurisdiction. Once he has made this distinction, however, he inexplicably reverts to territoriality. Secondly, whether the jurisdiction be construed as geographical or topographical, this belief is not a standing element in Aramean theology. Otherwise, they would not have attacked in the hill country during the first campaign, but would have stayed on the plains. Their explanation is a tidy bit of theological invention to rationalise the defeat.

To support SLSW, this passage would actually need to affirm the inverse of what it teaches. The Arameans think that Jehovah is territorial and they are proven wrong. To be useful to SLSW, they would need to view their own deity as territorial, and be proven correct (for example, by winning the second battle on the plains). Their willingness to attack in the hills initially refutes the idea that they view their own god as territorial. Their defeat on the plains refutes their explanation that Jehovah is territorial. As the Lord explains through his prophet: 'Because the Arameans think the LORD is a god of the hills and not a god of the valleys, I will deliver this vast army into your hands' (1 Kgs 20:26-28). God is universally sovereign; their gods are universally impotent. There is no territoriality here.

Summary

The Old Testament evidence is notable for how little it explains, and how much remains uncertain. Does every nation in the world have a ruling spirit? If so, do larger regions (such as continents) or smaller areas (such as towns) also have guardian spirits? Are these rulers invariably (or commonly) demonic? Is their jurisdiction geopolitical or ethnic? Does their territory expand or contract with the changing fortunes of the earthly political powers? Just about the only certainty is that the spirits are not geographically specific.

On a positive note, the most that can be inferred from these passages, and with some remaining uncertainties, is that city-states, nations or empires which opposed ancient Israel were serving as instruments of Satan against the people of God. Beyond this, the Old Testament sheds little light on the taxonomy of the demonic world.

The main reason for this relative silence about ruling demons is simply that there is 'no hint in the Old Testament of an alien order of spirits or demons with a rival realm outside the Lord's dominion.'[100] The Old Testament reflects a remarkable indifference towards angelology and demonology for the simple reason that it is preoccupied with the overpowering majesty of the sovereign God.[101] Thus, Di Lella notes that the concept of patron deities over each nation is modified within monotheistic Judaism: the guardian spirits are subject to divine authority, whether they seek to defy his will or to serve his purposes.[102] This is undoubtedly the most important lesson in spiritual warfare to be learned from the Old Testament.

RULING SPIRITS IN THE NEW TESTAMENT

Satan and his minions come into their own in the New Testament. Thus we might expect to see much more attention given to ruling demons. Such is not the case, however.

Instead, the concept develops in two directions. On the one hand, a few passages refer generally to spirits ruling the world. On the other, demons are occasionally linked to earthly bureaucratic structures which persecute the Church. Striking by its absence is any suggestion that the nations or regions of the world are divided into separate units, with each assigned to a particular demon.

Spirits Ruling the World

Hebrews 2:5 appears to assume that this world, unlike the world to come, is subject to the angels: 'It is not to angels that he has subjected the world to come;' presumably it is to angels that he has subjected this world. But Hebrews says nothing about different angels ruling over specific nations, nor does it indicate that these angels are fallen.

Ephesians uses a number of terms for demonic spirits, including 'world rulers' (Eph 6:12). But Paul never indicates that individual spirits are linked with particular nations. He finds it sufficient to affirm that Satan is the ruler of the kingdom of the air (Eph 2:2), and that the rulers and authorities are in the heavenly places (Eph 3:10; 6:12). The celestial nature of these spirits is emphasised, but nothing at all is said of specific and individualised earthly attachments.

Territorial Demons?

For the latter, proponents commonly cite four other references: the Legion of Mark 5, Artemis of Acts 19, the residence of Satan in Revelation 2:13, and the harlot of Revelation 17. None bears up to scrutiny.

'Do Not Send Us Out of the Area'

When Jesus was about to exorcise the Legion from the Gerasene demoniac, the demon begged repeatedly not to be sent 'out of the area' (Mark 5:10). Why? Often it is suggested, because he would be punished by his superiors if he lost control over his assigned territory.[103] Luke offers a different explanation: 'They begged him repeatedly not to order them to go into the Abyss' (Luke 8:31). The demons were afraid not of deportation, but of torment in hell (see also Mark 5:7).

Artemis of the Ephesians

Later, during Paul's mission in Ephesus, crowds of idol worshippers rioted, shouting: 'Great is Artemis of the Ephesians!' (Acts 19:28). Given this description, many conclude that she is a territorial spirit.[104]

Yet the deity worshipped as Artemis was actually an amalgamation of several originally distinct deities: the 'mother goddess' of Asia Minor, the Greek goddess Artemis, and the Roman goddess Diana. If deities from three distinct geographical regions could fuse, clearly none of their worshippers viewed them as geographically specific.

By Paul's time the worship of Artemis was no longer confined to any geographical, geopolitical, or ethnic boundary, but had spread to at least 33 other locations throughout the Mediterranean world. Simultaneously, Ephesus imported several dozen foreign deities from a comparably wide range of regions. Both practices demonstrate that there is no concept of ruling demons here: the Ephesians were simple polytheists.[105]

What, then, did the mob mean when it chanted, 'Great is Artemis of the Ephesians' (Acts 19:34)? Luke leaves us in no doubt, explaining the slogan in the very next verse. In the words of the city official, 'Men of Ephesus, doesn't all the world know that the city of Ephesus is the guardian of the temple of the great Artemis and of her image, which fell from heaven?' (Acts 19:35). Artemis was 'of the Ephesians' in that her central temple was located in the city. But that did not make the goddess guardian of the city. Just the opposite; it meant that the city was guardian of the goddess!

The Place Where Satan Dwells

The appeal to Revelation 2:13 fares no better. Despite the identification of Pergamum as the place where Satan lives and has his throne, this cannot possibly be an example of a spirit which reigns over an 'assigned territory'.[106]

In the first place, Satan is not meant to be a territorial spirit; he is the ruler over all territorial spirits. This is actually rather a pity, for if he were the spirit over Pergamum, the rest of the world could breathe considerably easier, since they would be free from his attack. Even Pergamum would not have it so bad, though, for a spirit's power is reflected in the breadth of its territory. Any spirit that reigns over a town as modest as Pergamum is not especially formidable.

Not only is the theory internally inconsistent, but its appeal to this verse runs afoul of the immediate context. The preoccupation with

Pergamum is puzzling, given the similar comments made about Smyrna, Thyatira and Philadelphia. Smyrna and Philadelphia each contain a 'synagogue of Satan' (Rev 2:9; 3:9), while Thyatira is 'where Satan's secrets' are taught within the Church (Rev 2:24). By the logic of SLSW, if Satan resides in Pergamum but works in Smyrna, Thyatira and Philadelphia, he does a fair bit of commuting! Besides, if he is ruler of Pergamum, what is he doing interfering in the other cities? Of course this is all rather silly, but it demonstrates the absurdity of the woodenly literalistic interpretative method employed to substantiate SLSW.

Significantly, each of these references to Satan points to a source of opposition against the church. In Smyrna and Philadelphia, the synagogues instigated persecution against the Christians. In this sense the Jews served as instruments of Satan, furthering his evil designs (Rev 2:9-10; 3:8-10).

In Thyatira, the threat to the church came from within, from a prophetess who encouraged participation in temple feasts, where sexual immorality and idolatry were rife (Rev 2:20-24). The character and effects of the teaching disclosed its Satanic origins.

Finally, in Pergamum the believers faced pressure to renounce Christ, and one member was martyred. This city contained a massive temple to Zeus (among other temples to other deities), was the centre for the healing cult of Asclepius with its snake symbol, and was the focus of emperor worship throughout the entire province.[107] It is not clear which of these institutions was the prime mover in the persecution, but any of them could justify the ascription: 'where Satan lives.'

So none of these descriptions supports the concept of geographically-restricted or fixed demonic spirits. Each merely identifies Satan as the ultimate source of persecution against the Church. The devil does not dwell physically or exclusively in any one city, temple or synagogue. Rather, he is at work anywhere that the church faces persecution without or corruption within.

Ironically, the only indisputable guardian spirits in these chapters are widely overlooked: the angels over the seven churches (Rev 1:20; 2:1,8,12,18; 3:1,7,14). Perhaps the reason for the neglect is that they are angelic not demonic, and rule over churches, not geographical regions. In any event, it is poignant testimony to the blinding force of presuppositions that the desired evidence can be found where it does not exist, while explicit and repeated evidence which does not fit the theory is overlooked.

The Whore Who Sits on Many Waters

Wagner describes this creature as 'the most influential territorial spirit mentioned in Scripture' and 'the most explicit New Testament example .... of a demonic spirit controlling nations and peoples.'[108] The argument hinges on the description of the harlot as sitting on 'many waters' (Rev 17:1), which represent many 'peoples, multitudes, nations and languages' (Rev 17:15).

The difficulty with this text is just the opposite of the preceding passage. Previously, Satan was held to be a territorial spirit over only one city. Now the harlot is purported to be a territorial spirit over many nations and peoples. This is no less problematic. If the authority of this creature encompasses many nations, then she may be a universal – or empire-wide – spirit, but she is not territorial. Moreover, her domain encompasses 'peoples', 'nations', and 'languages', not geographical regions. So she may be a universal *ethnic, geopolitical* or *linguistic* spirit; but she is not *geographical*!

The identification of the harlot as a territorial spirit is, of course, another example of excessive literalism, emphasising the particular form of expression in a way which misconstrues the obvious sense of it. 'Peoples, multitudes, nations and languages' (Rev 17:15) is a common phrase in Revelation for universality (Rev 5:9; 7:9; 11:9; 13:7; 14:6; also 10:11; 17:15). The apostle John does not attempt to distinguish the various categories. He uses multiple terms synonymously in order to emphasise comprehensiveness.[109]

If anything, SLSW must restrict the harlot's territory to the city of Rome. She rides on a beast with seven heads; the heads represent Rome, a city built on seven hills (Rev 17:9). At the end of the chapter, John makes the identification explicit: 'The woman ... is the great city that rules over the kings of the earth' (Rev 17:18). The city is Rome, which rules over an entire empire. Were she geographically specific, she would not rule over many peoples, nations and languages, or even over many territories. She would rule over Rome alone.

So the harlot of Revelation 17 fails as a territorial demon on all counts. She rules over numerous peoples, nations and language groups, not over a single fixed geographical region. She is a symbol not for a demon, but for a city. She is not territorial, but imperialistic.

A little background information clarifies John's point. In the ancient world, as in the modern, political powers used religion to reinforce their authority and to unite their subjects. Thus, in the lands which

Rome conquered, the military powers introduced the worship of the goddess Roma, alongside the deities already worshipped locally. Worship of Roma was not meant to supplant other deities, but was a unifying point for the entire empire, and served as an affirmation of loyalty to the political order.[110]

Revelation, however, vociferously rejects both the sovereignty claimed by Rome and the worship claimed by Roma. In a breathtaking challenge to the political ambitions and religious pretensions of the empire, John rejects the ascription of deity to Roma: she is not a goddess; she is a whore![111] His intention is not to affirm territoriality, but to reject idolatry and political tyranny.

AN ALTERNATIVE PROPOSAL

To keep this survey from being entirely negative in its conclusions, perhaps a tentative hypothesis is admissible. It can never be more than a hunch, because it lacks explicit biblical support. But it does at least assemble all the relevant data into a coherent picture.

The only probable ruling demons in the Old Testament are the 'princes' of Persia and Greece, which attack Israel (Dan 10:13, 20). The closest parallels to ruling demons in the New Testament are the references to Satan in Revelation, where he is associated with the forces which persecute the church, whether they be religious, as in Smyrna (2:9) and Philadelphia (3:9), political, as in Pergamum (2:13) or Rome (17:9, 18), or cultic, as in Thyatira (2:24).

The parallel and the divergence are suggestive. Tutelary malefactors appear in each passage. In Daniel, the demons (like the opposing angels) are assigned to geopolitical units. In Revelation, on the other hand, Satan is credited with a variety of activities which threaten the churches (whom the angels protect).

The hypothesis, then, is this: the concept of tutelary demons affirms simply that Satan lies behind any sort of opposition to the people of God. In Old Testament times, when the people of God constituted the nation of Israel, Satan worked through military conflict initiated by other, rival nations. Now that the locus of divine activity has shifted to the universal church, Satan works through a variety of other channels, both internal (such as heresy) and external (such as political oppression or religious competition).[112]

The structure of the demonic opposition then is largely derivative, reflecting the structure of the people of God at the time. Whatever form the adversity may take, that hostility is not merely of human origin, but is the work of Satan.

This principle can easily be transferred to the contemporary world. The point is not that each church, religion or nation is assigned to the jurisdiction of a specific demon. Rather, in so far as organisations or individuals oppose the people and work of God, they are serving as instruments of Satan. This much the Bible clearly affirms. More than this is speculation.

If this hypothesis is valid, then the attempt to delimit demonic jurisdictions is both futile and unnecessary. And if this is true of demons purportedly ruling over nations, the attempt to identify subordinate demons over regions, cities, towns and neighbourhoods has even less justification.

The Bible shows little interest in the taxonomy of the demonic world. It merely affirms that opposition to the work and people of God is Satanic in origin.[113] This is intended to serve as a counter to apostasy, and as motivation for perseverance, not as stimulus for 'spiritual mapping'.

CHAPTER THREE

THE WAR OF THE WORLDS: CONQUERING THE POWERS OF DARKNESS

Summary: The Bible does not call us to attack ruling demons; in fact, it warns us not to. Nor need we do so, for God has already defeated them in Christ.

The theory of territorial spirits is not necessarily linked with the practice of warfare prayer, but the two are normally combined. Even the standard terminology unites the two: 'strategic-level spiritual warfare'. This is a new sort of spiritual warfare ('warfare prayer') designed specifically to deal with strategic-level ('territorial') spirits.

To recall, warfare prayer consists of one fundamental characteristic, aggression, and two basic practices: naming the spirits, and using the names in direct confrontation and imprecation in an attempt to 'bind' the spirits. This chapter calls all this into question. The next chapter seeks to uncover what our role actually is.[114]

ATTACKING THE POWERS OF DARKNESS?

Wagner refers to what is becoming an increasingly common practice, when he asks: 'What happens when Christians shout, "I bind you, Satan!"?' His answer reflects sensitivity to biblical teaching: 'Perhaps not as much as we would hope. Satan will eventually be bound for 1,000 years, but it will be an angel who does it, not a human being (see Rev 20:1-2).' At the same time, he encourages sympathetic understanding of the practice: 'I would not be among those who scold brothers and sisters who aggressively rebuke the devil.'[115]

Assuming that such practices are somewhat over-enthusiastic, can they be viewed with condescension? Are they benign? What about other forms of aggressive confrontation with ruling spirits, as advocated – but not described – by Wagner?[116]

The Old Testament Evidence
The Old Testament provides little evidence of aggressive warfare against ruling spirits for the simple reason that God is always the one who subdues them (see, for example, Ps 82:6-8; Isa 24:21-22).

Warfare Prayer in Daniel?
Of all the Old Testament texts, only Daniel 10 has any human participants at all. But did Daniel engage in warfare prayer? Wagner has no doubt about it: this account 'shows us clearly that the only weapon Daniel had to combat these rulers of darkness was warfare prayer.'[117] This assessment deserves a second look.

Daniel never seeks the names of the demons or the angels, nor does he ever use them in prayer. The names are given in an offhand fashion in the course of explaining the delay in answering his earlier prayer

(Dan 10:13,20). Moreover, the only names he receives are those of Gabriel and Michael, the angels helping Israel (8:16; 9:21; 10:13,21; 12:1). The evil spirits are known only by generic titles, 'prince of Persia' and 'prince of Greece' (10:20). If this passage teaches the importance of names, it is angelic names which are consequential. Generic titles are sufficient for demons (for example, 'prince of Norway', or 'spirit of ethnic Lithuanians'). Obtaining these requires neither special insight nor prolonged periods of prayer and fasting.

The use of generic titles poses another problem for those who advocate naming demons. Often the contemporary search for names leads into research of native religions, national characteristics and local history. These sources are meant to provide clues to the identity and function of the prevailing spirits. So, for example, Kali is often taken to be one of the ruling spirits over the land of India or over ethnic Indians; materialism is understood to be a ruling spirit over the Chinese, especially in the modernising countries of East Asia; while the spirit of violence is often held responsible for the chaos of American cities. Yet while Daniel reflects knowledge of the indigenous religions and culture, his names for the ruling spirits reveal none of this. All he offers is the generic 'prince of' Persia or Greece.

Thus, Keil describes the prince of Persia as 'the supernatural spiritual power standing behind the national gods, which we may properly call the guardian spirit of this kingdom.'[118] While the national gods are many and their names would be familiar to Daniel, the title given is singular and generic. This is not any one god, nor even the leading god of the Persian pantheon. The 'prince' of Persia is a general term for the 'supernatural spiritual power standing *behind* the national gods' (emphasis added). This is a far cry from naming the spirits and identifying their functions.

By the end of the account, it becomes clear why Daniel does not seek the names of either angels or demons: he does not need them. Daniel never rebukes the demons. In chapter 10, he prays merely for the explanation of a dream. Once he receives the interpretation – with the angel names and demon titles – he ceases praying (10:2-3). Elsewhere, he prays routinely (6:10), and he prays to meet crisis needs (such as, to receive the interpretation of occasional visions, 2:18-19; 9:3-4, 20-23; 10:2-3,12-14). But he never practices warfare prayer. Only one extended prayer is recorded in the book, and that is a prayer of confession and repentance (9:2-23).

Nor does the angel ever suggest that the proper sort of prayer would weaken the ruling demons or put an end to the oppression of Israel. The vision concerns 'what will happen ... in the future' (10:14). Daniel anticipates the future, he does not change it, 'for what has been determined must take place' (11:36), including a period of unprecedented suffering (11:28-35; 12:1). Persecution comes despite the power of God and the intervention of the archangel Michael, and there is no suggestion that any human intervention would change anything. God's people will not be delivered from suffering, but will be delivered through it (12:2-3).

In an article on the theme of God as warrior, Hiebert captures well the thrust of the entire book: 'The victory is so exclusively attributed in these visions to the divine warrior that the author appears to renounce any human participation in the conflict.'[119] If anything, then, Daniel is an example of how not to conduct warfare prayer.[120]

Wagner himself concedes the point in an earlier book, and then again in a later book. Distinguishing between the traditional cautious approach to spiritual warfare and the more aggressive pattern of warfare prayer, he acknowledges that Daniel fits into the former.

> Daniel did not engage the enemy directly. In fact, he apparently did not even know a battle was taking place.... Appropriate caution, then, is called for in all spiritual warfare.[121]

Similarly, in his most recent book on this theme, he writes, 'This chapter [Dan 10] does not provide a method for conducting spiritual warfare.'[122]

At the same time, Wagner suggests that alongside the passivity of Daniel, 'there seems to be a concomitant biblical mandate for boldness in engaging the enemy.'[123] So the survey continues, in hopes of uncovering such a mandate.

Warfare Prayer Elsewhere in the Old Testament?

The closest that the Old Testament comes to aggressive warfare against the demons is an incident described in Zechariah 3:1-2:

> Joshua the high priest [was] standing before the angel of the LORD, and Satan [was] standing at his right side to accuse him. The [angel of the] LORD said to Satan, 'The LORD rebuke you, Satan! The LORD ... rebuke you!'

Two features of this incident are particularly significant. First of all, the only human participant, Zechariah, is merely a bystander and an observer; it is an angel which confronts Satan. Secondly, the angel does not directly rebuke the devil; instead, he appeals to God to do so. So if a mandate for aggressive warfare prayer appears anywhere in Scripture, it must be in the New Testament.

The New Testament Teaching

Between the Old and New Testaments, the text from Zechariah was quoted in a Jewish writing called 'The Assumption of Moses'.[124] According to this tradition, when Moses died, Satan tried to claim authority over the body because Moses had murdered an Egyptian. The archangel Michael refused to permit this. But instead of engaging Satan in argument or in battle, he merely countered with the words of Zechariah 3:2, 'The Lord rebuke you!'

The details of this intertestamental text need not detain us, nor do we need to assume that the story records an historical incident.[125] What is instructive is the application of the story in Jude 8-10. Jude uses the account to chide some of his readers who deride spirits (verse 8). The apostle does not provide much information about their motives or their denunciations. But first-century Jewish curses against the devil have survived the intervening centuries and give us some idea of what was probably occurring.

The ascetic Jewish community at Qumran incorporated curses against Satan and the demons alongside praise to God in their worship:

> Blessed be the God of Israel for all His holy purpose and for His works of truth! ... Cursed be Satan for his sinful purpose and may he be execrated for his wicked rule! Cursed be all the spirits of his company for their ungodly purpose and may they be execrated for all their service of uncleanness! (1QM xiii)

In another liturgical curse from Qumran, the worshippers addressed Satan directly:

> Be cursed, Angel of Perdition and Spirit of Destruction, in all the thoughts of your guilty inclination and all your abominable plots and your wicked design, and may you be damned ... Amen, amen. (4Q286-87; see also 4Q280-82)

Ritual cursing of the devil and his demons was a routine element in the worship of the Qumran community.

Jude rebukes this sort of imprecation. If anyone has both the authority and the power to be contemptuous of spiritual beings, Michael does. After all, he is the righteous and mighty archangel, engaged in a divinely commissioned task, serving as guardian angel of the Jewish people and appointed to be the chief opponent of the devil (Dan 10:13,21; 12:1; 1 Enoch 20:5; 40:4-9).

Yet despite his righteousness, his power, his commission, and his authority, 'even the archangel Michael, when he was disputing with the devil about the body of Moses, did not dare to bring a slanderous accusation against him, but said, "The Lord rebuke you!" Yet these men speak abusively against whatever they do not understand' (Jude 9-10).

The point is two-fold. For one, if the great archangel is so circumspect with the devil, how much more prudent should mere mortals be with demons. For the other, it is God alone who has the authority and power to rebuke Satan and the demons; mortal man does not.[126]

Though his readers claim prophetic insight to justify their actions (Jude 8), Jude censures them for arrogance. Like Michael, we may beseech God to rebuke ruling demons, but we must not assume the authority to do that ourselves; nor dare we mock or revile them.[127]

Wagner denies the relevance of this passage on two grounds.[128] First, it applies only to invective against Satan himself, not to that directed against Satan's subordinates. Secondly, it derives from, and therefore applies to, only those living in Old Testament times, when 'believers were not given the same authority over the powers of evil that Jesus has given to us.'[129]

The problems with this rationale are obvious. Jude was addressing his own contemporaries, not Old Testament believers: 'These men speak abusively against whatever they do not understand.... These men are blemishes at your love feasts' (Jude 10,12). Jude intends the rebuke for the Christian church, not for Old Testament times.

Nor is Jude restricting his comments to those who speak abusively against Satan. Admittedly he cites the example of the archangel Michael not slandering the devil, but this is argument by analogy. His opponents are more inclusive in their invective: 'these dreamers ... slander *celestial beings*' (Jude 8, emphasis added). So Jude explicitly warns humans not to indulge in tirades against either demons or Satan.

This admonition reappears in 2 Peter, where it is generalised. From a specific statement about an incident in the ministry of the archangel Michael, it becomes a general proposition referring to all angels in their dealings with demons, but the application remains the same.[130]

> Bold and arrogant, these men are not afraid to slander celestial beings; yet even angels, although they are stronger and more powerful, do not bring slanderous accusations against such beings in the presence of the Lord. But these men blaspheme in matters they do not understand (2 Pet 2:10-12).

A more explicit caution against aggressively confronting demons is hard to imagine; a stronger warning would seem necessary.

THE DEFEAT OF THE POWERS OF DARKNESS
If we lack the power and authority to challenge ruling demons, does this mean that we are at their mercy? Not at all. The consistent testimony of the New Testament is that Christ has already decisively defeated them. The apostle Paul provides the fullest exposition of this point, and he does so in his letter to the Ephesians.

Demons in Ephesus
Paul's teaching in Ephesians is best seen in the light of his earlier ministry in Ephesus, recorded in Acts 19. Here we learn of the Ephesians' early experience with demons and of their futile attempts to defend themselves through the use of magic. Through successful and through failed exorcisms, the Ephesians learn of the power of the Lord at work in the gospel and through the apostle.

Warfare Prayer in Ephesus: Yes, No, Maybe?
According to Wagner, Acts 19 provides 'the most outstanding example' of the apostle Paul engaging in strategic-level spiritual warfare.[131]

> The major key to opening Ephesus and Asia Minor to the gospel was not brilliant preaching or persuasive words of human wisdom, but spiritual warfare on all levels, including strategic-level spiritual warfare.[132]

The use of warfare prayer in Ephesus was the key to his 'greatest missionary and evangelistic success'; the neglect of warfare prayer in Athens was the key to his 'greatest evangelistic failure'.[133]

On second thought, though, perhaps Paul did not employ strategic-level spiritual warfare in Ephesus:

> As far as we know from Luke's account in Acts, in Ephesus, Paul overtly engaged in spiritual warfare on the ground level and on the occult level, but not on the strategic level.... We can surmise, then, that Paul did not have a head-on encounter with Diana [the purported territorial spirit] in Ephesus.[134]

If Paul did not confront the strategic-level spirit over Ephesus, how can this non-event be an instance of strategic-level spiritual warfare? Because 'often significant damage is done on the strategic level to territorial spirits through power ministries on the ground and occult levels.'[135]

The implications of this concession should not be missed. Paul's greatest evangelistic success, and his triumph over one of the most powerful territorial spirits in the ancient world, purportedly came without warfare prayer.

> Without overtly confronting Diana herself, Paul and the missionaries had weakened her authority.... The result was that the kingdom of God came to Ephesus and the surrounding area of Asia Minor in a more widespread and more notable way than any other place in which Paul had ministered.[136]

If so much can be achieved without warfare prayer, what more is there to gain by its use? If spectacular success comes without warfare prayer, how can failure be attributed to neglecting it? If 'the most outstanding example' of warfare prayer provides no actual evidence of its use, then what indication is there that Paul ever employed it?

Magic and Power in Ephesus
Though not in the sense proposed by Wagner, the incidents of Acts 19 are actually significant for understanding the practice of spiritual warfare, and especially for appreciating the message of Ephesians. But the focus of attention should be on the first, not the second, half of the chapter.

In total, Paul spent more than two years in Ephesus, teaching, healing and casting out demons, even at a distance (Acts 19:1-12). But apparently the greatest impetus to the conversion of the Ephesians did not come from any of this. Rather, it came from a failed exorcism performed by Jews.

The seven sons of Sceva, Jewish exorcists, invoke the name of Jesus to cast out a demon. Instead of obeying, the demon responds, 'Jesus I know, and I know about Paul, but who are you?', and then proceeds to beat them bloody (Acts 19:15). Notably, this brings great respect to the cause of Christ, and causes many converts to confess their participation in magical rites. When they come together to burn their magic charms and scrolls, their value was in excess of 125 years' salary for the average worker (Acts 19:17-20).

But what has a failed exorcism to do with magic? In the first century, sorcery relied on powerful names. Any number of names might be invoked by a magician in a charm. The only necessary qualification was that the name be thought to have spiritual power. Thus, ancient charms might invoke the names of a wide variety of deities, including Greek, Roman and Egyptian gods, as well as the Jewish designation, Yahweh.[137]

Against this background the events of Acts 19 make sense. The seven sons of Sceva, seeing Paul employ the name of Jesus to good effect, decide to incorporate that name in their exorcism. They quickly find out, however, that the power lies not in the name, but in the person of Jesus. Their failure demonstrates that Paul is not employing a Christian form of magic, but something far more powerful: he is calling upon the true God and is being heard. Seeing the failure of sorcery but the power of the gospel, many bystanders renounce magic and come to faith.

This raises painful questions for contemporary practitioners who stress the importance of names in spiritual warfare. If the key to power does not rest in using the name of Jesus, how much less can it depend on using the names of demons! The reliance on names finds a closer parallel in first-century magic than in biblical Christianity.[138]

The Fear of Demons in Ephesus
The incident in Ephesus also provides an important background to understanding Paul's subsequent letter. Ephesians contains proportionately more references to demons and to power than any book in the New Testament.[139] The reason is not hard to find.

The Ephesians had always lived in fear of demons; thus their reliance upon magic for protection. But in their initial enthusiasm for the gospel, they renounced the worship of spirits and burned their magic books. This seemed safe enough while Paul was in their midst. Yet suddenly he was gone (Acts 20:1).

Any contemporary convert from animism can appreciate the Ephesians' predicament. Their conversion would have angered the spirits; they rightly worried that the demons would seek vengeance. (The treatment received by the seven sons of Sceva was clear evidence of the spirits' power and malice.) Previously they had their charms, incantations, and amulets to protect them. Now, by renouncing both the worship of spirits and the use of magic, they have managed at one and the same time to antagonise the spirits and to take away their customary form of protection. Worse still, the apostle who had demonstrated power over demons had left them for ministry elsewhere. Many converts from animism have renounced their faith and returned to demon worship under less pressure. Would the Ephesians hold firm or fall back?

To quell their fear, Paul does not provide them with a sure-fire technique for conquering spirits. Instead, he draws their attention to the victory which God has already won over the demons.

The Defeat of Demons in Ephesians 1-3
Discussions of spiritual warfare generally concentrate on Ephesians 6. This is unfortunate, because the later exhortations rely on the foundation laid in the first three chapters. Here Paul identifies three arenas in which God has already decisively defeated the demons. The first consists of the resurrection and exaltation of Jesus (1:18-21). The second comes in the conversion of individuals (2:1-6). The third comprises the incorporation of Gentiles into the people of God (3:8-11). Through Christ, God has demonstrated his power over all the machinations of the evil one, including death, rebellion and deception.

The Exaltation of Christ and the Defeat of Demons
In Ephesians 1:20-21 Paul describes the resurrection and exaltation of Christ as a victory over demons:

> [God] raised him from the dead and seated him at his right hand in the heavenly realms, far above all rule and authority, power and dominion, and every title that can be given, not only in the present age but also in the one to come.

Jesus is now seated, at the right hand of God, in the heavenly realms, far above the spirits.

All four descriptions emphasise his authority: in ancient times, kings

would sit on the throne when holding court, and they were often represented as being at the right hand of the deity, in the position of greatest
power and highest honour.[140] Christ, seated at the right hand of God,
has already begun to reign as king in the heavenlies, and the evil spirits
are included among his subjects.

His kingdom is cosmic in scope. All spiritual beings are under his
authority, whether rule, authority, power, dominion, or whatever other
title they might be given (1:21a). The significance of the last phrase is
easily missed in translation. In a culture which emphasises the power
of names, and which believes that knowledge of spirit names brings
power over them, Paul proclaims Christ to be superior to 'every name
which can be named' (1:21a, author's translation).[141] The authority of
Christ includes every realm where the demons might possibly be found,
whether in this age or the age to come (1:21b).

Paul is heaping up synonyms to make a point: Christ rules over
every conceivable demon, named or unnamed, in heaven or on earth,
in this age or the one to come. But these are not abstract theological
statements about Christ. They have direct ramifications for his followers: the power of Christ is at work for them (1:19); the authority
of Christ is exercised on their behalf (1:22). This power is not only
great, it is incomparably great (1:19a). The power at work on their
behalf is equivalent to the power which exalted Christ not only above,
but far above, all the spirits of heaven and earth (1:20). What the
power did for him it will do for them.

Four Greek words are used for this power: *dunamis, energeia,
kratos, isxus*. Significantly, all are used in the ancient magical papyri to
describe the power of the spirits and the magicians who call upon
them.[142] Such power belongs not to the spirits or to their mediums,
Paul insists, but to Christ, who uses it for the benefit and protection of
his followers.

The Salvation of Christians and the Defeat of Demons
The second battlefield on which God has defeated the demons is the
salvation of each convert. Each person who turns to Christ marks a modest,
but unmistakable, break in the control of the demons over the world.

In 2:1-6, Paul looks back on the pre-Christian experience of the
Ephesians. When they did not know and serve God, they were controlled by three other forces: the world, the flesh and the devil. They
followed the ways of the world (2:1). They lived in submission to the

ruler of the demonic realm ('the realm of the air'), the spirit who continues to work in those who are disobedient (2:2). They served the lusts of the flesh, fulfilling its desires and thoughts (2:3).

As a result, they were dead in transgression and sin (2:1), and were under the wrath of God (2:3). But God raised them from death to life with Christ (2:5). In fact, he did more than this. He also exalted them with Christ, and seated them with him in the heavenlies, where Christ is (2:6).[143] That is to say, seated with Christ in the heavenlies, the Ephesian converts are now above all demons (see also 1:21).

In Colossians 2 Paul returns to this idea. In their pre-Christian state, the Colossians were subject to the evil spirits, and were thus prisoners of the kingdom of darkness (Col 2:15; 1:13). But on the cross, Christ defeated the demonic powers: 'Disarming the rulers and authorities, God exposed them publicly, leading them in his triumphal procession in Christ' (Col 2:15, author's translation). Like a conquering general, God leads the vanquished demons in a triumphal procession, demonstrating his prowess through the abject humiliation of his opponents. The forces of evil are not merely defeated; they are mocked and derided.[144] In the process, God liberated his people from demonic tyranny, and brought them into the kingdom ruled by his Son (Col 1:13).

The Universal Church and the Defeat of Demons

God's triumph over Satan does more than bring salvation to individual Christians. It also brings them together into one body, whether Jew or Gentile (Eph 3:6).

What does this have to do with spiritual warfare? Just this: by means of this reconstituted people of God, the wisdom of God is now revealed to the rulers and authorities in the heavenly realms (Eph 3:10).

Until the resurrection of Christ, Satan had ample reason to boast. The only people who professed allegiance to the true God was a small and unimportant ethnic group, restricted to a provincial outpost on the edge of the Mediterranean Sea, and insignificant on the political stage. The rest of the world appeared to be firmly within the kingdom of darkness. Now the church has exploded across all boundaries, and incorporates all peoples. Entire ethnic groups and nations which were previously consigned to the darkness have now entered the light.

Thus, by its very existence as one people, the church proclaims the wisdom of God to the rulers and authorities in the heavenlies (Eph 3:10). As Lincoln observes, 'The Church provides hostile cosmic powers with a tangible reminder that their authority has been decisively broken and that all things are subject to Christ.'[145]

Implications for SLSW

Satan is powerful, SLSW warns; he holds most of the world in darkness. Its liberation depends on us, and the use of warfare prayer.[146] Paul contradicts both propositions.

First, he insists, the power of Satan has already been decisively broken. The proof of this is found in the resurrection of Jesus, our own salvation and the existence of a universal church.

We need not fear Satan's power: Christ has much greater power, and far higher authority. That power is at work for us. That authority is exercised on our behalf (Eph 1:18-21).

Nor need we fear Satan's vengeance. His authority over us was never derived from the geographical region where we lived, but from the way that we lived. Now our sin has been forgiven in Christ, and we are free from his domain (Eph 2:1-6; Col 1:13; 2:13-15).

Nor need we fear Satan's dominion over the world. His authority has been decisively broken and the kingdom of God has triumphed. The inclusion of Gentiles in the church is proof enough of that (Eph 3:6-10).

Secondly, all this was done without our help or involvement. In fact, it was all accomplished by God, in Christ, while we were still slaves of Satan, imprisoned in darkness. The war has been won, and it has been won without us.

CONCLUSION

At least some proponents of SLSW try to incorporate Paul's perspective. Wagner, for instance, comments:

> Many raise questions about the appropriateness of taking the spiritual offensive against principalities and powers because of the Bible's teaching that they have already been defeated.
> Nothing, of course, can be added to the blood of Jesus shed on the cross. His sacrifice was made once and for all. Satan has been defeated. Jesus has overcome the world. The outcome of the war is no longer in doubt. But meanwhile we are engaged in mop-up operations.[147]

This sounds fine in principle, but in practice the victory of Christ over the demons receives little attention in SLSW, and would seem to require major changes in the expectations placed on warfare prayer.

The crucial question, perhaps, concerns the meaning of 'mop-up operations'. Wagner draws a parallel to the Emancipation Proclamation, enacted by Abraham Lincoln in the midst of the American Civil War.[148] While Lincoln declared African-Americans 'free' and gave them all the rights of full citizenship, Wagner observes, social equality was a rather remote goal for a long time afterwards.

If this analogy is appropriately chosen, then it reinforces the objection against SLSW. The Emancipation Proclamation accomplished next to nothing. At least, it actually freed no slaves. As President, Lincoln did not have legal authority to free the slaves. As Commander-in-Chief, he did have such authority, but only over lands occupied in war, and at this stage there were no occupied lands. It was another three years before the passage of the thirteenth amendment to the Constitution, prohibiting slavery throughout the country.[149] Even then, many areas enacted 'Jim Crow' laws, effectively curtailing the liberty so recently won, and former slaves were often reduced to tenant farming under exploitative conditions which guaranteed a life of perpetual indebtedness and oppression.

The question raised by this analogy, then, is whether the death of Christ amounts to nothing more than a declaration of intent, to be fulfilled at some indefinite time in the future when circumstances permit and as his people take charge over new territories, or whether it actually achieves an immediate and decisive change in the status and experience of believers.[150] According to New Testament scholar N. T. Wright:

> Because of what Jesus did on the cross, the powers and authorities are a beaten, defeated lot, so that (by implication) neither the Colossians nor anyone else who belongs to Jesus need be overawed by them again.[151]

The overall thrust of SLSW is markedly different from this, both in content and in tone.

This weakness cannot be overcome by merely affirming faith in the victory of Christ on the cross. No one doubts that proponents of SLSW believe this. The problem is a failure to integrate this belief with the theory and practice of spiritual warfare. Paul portrays the spirits as vanquished and captive; proponents of SLSW tell us that never in history have they been stronger.[152] These two perspectives cannot be integrated; whichever is endorsed, the other must be rejected.

CHAPTER FOUR

THE BATTLE CONTINUES: STANDING FIRM AGAINST THE POWERS OF DARKNESS

Summary: Though Satan has been decisively defeated, he is engaged in a desperate counterattack against the Church. Our role is to hold our ground in the strength provided through the use of traditional spiritual disciplines. We conquer Satan not by overwhelming all opposition to the gospel but by remaining firm in the face of opposition.

Martin Luther once likened his contemporaries to a drunken peasant astride a donkey: falling off one side, he remounts, only to slide off the other side. This same tendency plagues the practice of spiritual warfare.

On the one side are those who blissfully ignore Satan, either out of casual neglect or in the faint hope that if they do not bother him, he will not bother them. On the other side are those who pray in an attempt to defeat Satan or to free the world from his grasp. The latter implicitly deny the teaching of Ephesians 1–3, that God has conquered Satan already. The former implicitly reduce the wide range of biblical teaching to Ephesians 1–3, and presume that defeat renders Satan impotent.

Paul rejects the former no less than the latter. After proclaiming the defeat of the demonic powers (Eph 1–3), the apostle warns against the stratagems and assaults of the evil one (Eph 6:11,16). God has won the conclusive battle, obtained our freedom, and imparted his power to us. Now he calls us to join the war effort.

What sort of spiritual warfare is consistent with the defeat of Satan? Paul provides the answer in Ephesians 6:10-18.

STANDING OUR GROUND AGAINST THE DEVIL

Theologian Walter Wink insists that Christians are not to be passive in the battle against Satan: instead, 'Paul depicts the church taking the fight to the enemy.'[153]

But this confuses defence with passivity, and activity with aggression. Wink is right to insist that Paul rejects quietism and non-resistance. Christians are to be active in battle. But just as clearly, Ephesians 6:10-20 offers no support for launching an attack against Satan and his forces. There is a battle to be fought, but our role is neither to win some spectacular victory, nor even to launch an all-out offensive. Our function is primarily – if not exclusively – defensive.

Who Attacks Whom?

Paul does not exhort the Ephesian Church to launch an offensive against Satan; he urges them merely to stand firm in the face of attack. Four times in this paragraph, he exhorts them to hold their ground. 'Put on the full armour of God in order that you may be able to *stand*' (6:11); 'Take up the full armour of God, so that you may be able to *withstand* ... and having accomplished everything, to *stand*' (6:13); '*Stand*, then' (6:14, author's translation, emphasis added).

This exhortation is the main thrust of the entire paragraph.[154] All that precedes builds toward the exhortation: they are to be strong in the Lord and to put on the full armour of God *so that* they may be able to stand firm (6:10-11). All that follows reinforces the exhortation: the rest of the paragraph elaborates the spiritual disciplines which will *enable them* to stand (6:14-18). The preoccupation with subordinate details of armour and demons often distracts from the main point: 'Stand firm.'

The metaphor portrays soldiers, threatened by the enemy, and engaged in close combat. Under fierce assault, the commander does not order them to launch an offensive, but to hold their ground. 'It involves standing firm, holding one's position, resisting, not surrendering to the opposition but prevailing against it.'[155] It is a defensive – not an offensive – posture.

Confusion sometimes arises because of a misunderstanding of this metaphor in a military context. Wagner objects:

> Some, I believe, want to hope against hope that since Christ has defeated Satan on the cross, all we are expected to do is to 'stand'. If we stand around with our hands in our pockets, evil will somehow not bother us or our society.[156]

But when facing an enemy onslaught, 'stand' does not mean 'stand around with our hands in our pockets'. It means to hold the ground already taken in the face of an enemy counter-offensive. This is the appropriate stance for Christians: Christ has won the battle; we are to stand firm in the face of Satanic counter-attack.

'Stand' is a common exhortation in Paul's writings, and always carries a defensive connotation. The Thessalonians are urged to 'stand firm' in the midst of persecution (1 Thess 3:8) and in the face of false teaching (2 Thess 2:15). The Philippians are urged to 'stand firm' in the midst of persecution, and not to be cowed by fear of their opponents (Phil 1:27-28; also 4:1). Epaphras wrestles in prayer for the Colossians with the aim that they 'stand firm' in all the will of God, lest they be swayed by heresy or seduced by sin (Col 4:12). The particular danger in view differs in each instance, but the exhortation to 'stand' presupposes that the Christians are under attack; it does not call them to initiate an attack.[157]

Human Impotence

The entire passage presupposes the weakness of man in the face of demonic attack. This is the first note which Paul sounds, and he strikes it repeatedly, employing redundancy for emphasis: 'Be strong in the Lord and in the might of his strength' (6:10). Christians need power, might and strength; and they need them in the degree that only God can provide.

Twice Paul urges them to put on the 'full armour' of God (Eph 6:11,13). In the first century, as today, armament varied according to the degree of mobility or protection desired. 'Full armour' is the equipment of a heavily armed foot soldier, designed more for protection than for mobility.[158] The battle is fierce, the opponent is fearsome and the soldier is expected merely to hold his ground, not to advance. Under these circumstances, mobility is not necessary and light armour offers insufficient protection; heavy armour is needed.

So, too, this is the armour *of God*. At the very least, Paul means that the armour comes from God. We do not have strength in our own resources to withstand the enemy; it is God who provides the necessary weaponry. But Isaiah describes both God and the Messiah as bearing arms, and Paul seems to have taken much of his language from that source (Isa 11:4-5; 59:17). This raises the possibility of a fuller meaning: not only do Christians receive their armour from God; they actually wear his armour, by which he won the victory over Satan. As Lincoln notes, 'This would underline both the serious nature of the battle and the writer's belief that believers are only able to prevail through the protection and power of God himself.'[159]

Notably, the armour is consistently defensive. Belts, breastplates, sandals, shields, and helmets protect the soldier; they do not enable him to inflict wounds on his opponent. The only possibly offensive weapon is the sword, and even this can be used for self-protection as much as for attacking. Given that the sword represents the word of God, which Jesus used to defend himself against Satan's temptations (Matt 4:1-11; Luke 4:1-12), there is reason to believe that even this weapon is defensive.

The exhortation to take up these weapons demonstrates that Christians have an active role to play in the warfare, but this armament is better suited for defensive purposes than for vigorous assault. Both passivity and aggression are precluded.

Demonic Opposition

Christians need so much protection because of the identity of their opponents: rulers, authorities, world rulers of darkness, and spirits of evil in the heavenlies. These are not 'flesh and blood', but spirits (6:12). The implication is clear: were the opponents human, the Ephesians might have a fighting chance; unhappily, the opponents are supernatural, so the Christians are out of their league.

This is precisely why God provides the armour: 'Put on the full armour of God,' Paul urges, '*for* our struggle is not against flesh and blood' (6:12). Because the opponents are spirits, Paul exhorts, '*therefore* put on the full armour of God' (6:13). These are formidable opponents, far beyond the capabilities of mere mortals to defeat. The best we can hope to do is to hold our ground, but even this would be impossible without extensive assistance from God himself.

The activities of these spirits confirm that they are on the offensive against believers, rather than vice versa. It is Satan who schemes. Whether through head-on attacks or devious strategies, it is he who takes the initiative (6:11). The Christians do not train for 'the day of liberation'. Instead, they defend themselves on 'the evil day' (6:13). It is Satan who shoots fiery arrows at believers, and they who must protect themselves (6:16), not the reverse.

This portrait of the devil as the aggressive party is consistent with the other descriptions of him in the New Testament. James, for example, urges his readers 'to resist' the devil, not to attack him, with the promise that he will flee (Jas 4:7). The devil is on the prowl, like a hungry, roaring lion, Peter warns; he seeks someone to devour (1 Pet 5:8). Christians are not called to launch a pre-emptive strike. Instead, they are to resist and withstand him (1 Pet 5:9).

From this it is clear why Christians are not called to go on the offensive against Satan. The first reason is that God has already won the battle. The second is that demons are still a potent force. That is to say, there is no battle to win, and this is fortunate, for if there were, we could not win it.

It falls to us, however, to hold the ground which Christ won at such cost. As New Testament scholar Andrew Lincoln explains:

> The decisive victory has already been won by God in Christ, and the task of believers is not to win but to stand, that is, to preserve and maintain what has been won.... The major victory has been achieved, but...

believers must appropriate what has already been gained for them and do so against continuing assaults, and this is not automatic.[160]

This modest task is formidable enough, even with the strength and protection which come from God. To attempt more is both unnecessary (what more can be done than what Jesus has done?) and foolhardy (can mortals conquer spirits?).

The Place of Prayer in Warfare

As the warfare metaphor tapers off, Paul repeatedly calls the Ephesians to prayer: 'Pray in the Spirit on all occasions with all kinds of prayers and requests.... Always keep on praying for all the saints. Pray also for me.... Pray' (Eph 6:18-20). Is this warfare prayer?

Technically, while spiritual warfare and prayer are mentioned in adjoining verses (6:17,18), the two are not mingled. Grammatically, the two sections are related: 6:18 contains two participles but no main verb; thus, it is syntactically dependent on the earlier paragraph. But the exhortations to prayer (6:18-20) fall outside the warfare metaphor (6:10-17). Each piece of armour stands for a Christian characteristic or discipline; truth is the belt; righteousness, the breastplate; faith, a shield; and so on. Prayer is not related to any piece of armour.

Ironically, then, Ephesians 6:10-20 mentions both warfare and prayer, but never 'warfare prayer'. But, of course, the more important issue relates to practice not to terminology. On this matter warfare prayer fares no better.

Paul's concept of prayer is evident from two different angles: his requests for prayer in 6:18-20 and his actual recorded prayers earlier in the letter. Neither lends any support to the distinctive practices of warfare prayer.

Twice in this epistle Paul prays for the Ephesians, and once he requests their prayer for himself. In 1:17-19, Paul prays that the Spirit might lead the Ephesians into a deeper knowledge of God, including an awareness of the victory of God over the demons. In 3:14-19, he appeals to God for their strengthening, and for a growing awareness of the immeasurable love of Christ. Finally, in 6:18-20, he exhorts the Ephesians to pray, not just once but four times in three verses. In addition to urging general prayer for other Christians, he asks them to pray that he might preach accurately and fearlessly.

All of these prayers are rather traditional; there is nothing particularly bold or aggressive about them. Not once does Paul pray against Artemis, the alleged territorial spirit of Ephesus. Never does he ask them to pray against the ruling spirit over Rome, from where he is likely to have written this letter. He asks merely that they pray for other Christians as he was praying for them, and that they pray for him to be bold in evangelism.

Wagner is able to find warfare prayer here only by reading it into the text:

> What is the principal weapon of spiritual warfare that we need when we move into the evangelisation of our community? Prayer! .... The type of prayer most indicated for evangelism designed to take unbelievers from darkness to light and from the power of Satan to God is warfare prayer.[161]

The first half of the quote is supported by the text; the second is a gratuitous assumption. Four years later, when the key to effective ministry has shifted to pastors having personal intercessors, the meaning of 6:18-19 also shifts to support the new emphasis.[162]

These exhortations to prayer are also relevant to the issue of praying 'on site'. The very fact that Paul regularly prays for people several months' journey away, and requests their prayers for him, raises questions about any supposed advantages to praying on location. Apparently SLSW territorialises not only the demons, but also the power of God.

Summary
So on all counts, warfare prayer stands at odds with Paul's teaching on spiritual warfare. It minimises what Paul maximises: the victory which God has won over Satan. It counsels aggression whereas he exhorts to steadfastness. It relies on innovative technique, but Paul urges the practice of traditional spiritual disciplines. It promises great power to humans, while Paul warns concerning the abiding power of the demons. It invents a new form of prayer: aggression directed against demons; Paul practises the only sort of prayer found in Scripture: humble petition addressed to God.

But, of course, there is more in Scripture about spiritual warfare than what appears in Ephesians or even in Paul. In particular, Revelation reflects at length on our battle against Satan, and on methods for conquering him.

CONQUERING SATAN

If Ephesians were all we had to go on, we could conceivably grow complacent in the victory which Christ has won (Eph 1–3). Admittedly, Paul concludes his letter to the Ephesians with a sustained and emphatic reminder of the continued power and animosity of Satan against the Church (Eph 6:10-18). But this could be neglected given the earlier emphasis. After all, if Christ has defeated the demons, what is the urgency behind spiritual warfare?

Revelation answers this question. Significantly, the verb 'conquer' (*nikao*; NIV: 'overcome') appears seventeen times in Revelation, and only eleven times in the rest of the New Testament. Each of the letters to the seven churches promises a reward to those who 'conquer' (2:7; 2:11; 2:17; 2:26; 3:5; 3:12; 3:21; 21:7). Christ 'conquers' Satan (5:5; 17:14); Satan 'conquers' the church (6:2; 13:7); and the church 'conquers' Satan (12:11; 15:2). All this conquering is bound to shed light on the war between Satan and mankind, and how the devil and his forces can be conquered.

'Those Who Conquer'

Given the eight appearances of 'conquer' within Revelation 2-3, it comes as no surprise to be told that these chapters contain Jesus' 'most direct instructions' on SLSW.[163]

What is surprising, however, is that the attempt to find warfare prayer here requires an extended and convoluted argument involving a change of words (from *nikao* to *deo*) and a succession of three passages from the Gospels (Luke 11:22; Mark 3:27 and Matt 12:29; Matt 16:19).[164] This hardly qualifies for 'direct' instructions.

The first hint that this interpretation misses the point is the fact that it does not derive from Revelation 2–3. The second clue is that it depends not just on a single outside text, but an entire string of them.[165] Given that 'conquer' (*nikao*) appears more often in this one book than in all the rest of the New Testament combined, the meaning of the term in Revelation should be apparent from its use in these chapters.[166]

Each of the seven letters identifies a particular challenge which the Christians in that city must conquer. The Ephesians have forsaken their first love (2:4-5). The Christians in Smyrna face persecution (2:10), as do those in Philadelphia (3:8-9). The church in Pergamum is tempted to indulge in idol food, sexual immorality, and heresy (2:14-

15), as are the believers living in Thyatira (2:20-22). Those in Sardis are apathetic about their faith (3:2-3). The Laodiceans are arrogant yet impoverished (3:17-18).

Behind each of these adverse circumstances lurks Satan. He motivates the harassment experienced from the synagogue in Smyrna (2:9) and Philadelphia (3:9). He is the driving force behind the political persecution in Pergamum (2:13). He deceives the false teachers of Thyatira into promoting his 'so-called deeper teachings' (2:24).

In such situations, those who conquer are not people who bind Satan or overpower the territorial spirits. The victorious Christians are the ones who surmount the threats through faithfulness to the gospel and endurance in persecution.[167]

Admittedly this seems a strange meaning for 'conquer': not defeating an opponent, but enduring opposition and persecution. Yet this is precisely how Jesus conquered Satan.

The Lion-Lamb Conquers

The last of the seven exhortations portrays Christ as a model for how the church is to conquer its opponents, human or demonic:

> 'The one who conquers, to him I will give the right to sit with me on my throne, just as I also conquered and sat down with my Father on his throne' (3:21, author's translation).

Jesus is the pattern, both in the reward which awaits those who conquer, and in how they are to conquer.

Revelation 4–5 describes the reward which Jesus received and the method by which he conquered. Chapter four begins with a description of the majesty of God upon his throne (4:1-11). The latter half of chapter five picks up on this, portraying Christ's exaltation in even more glorious terms (5:7-14). This is the reward Christ receives for his conquering: he shares the glory of God.

In the intervening verses, 5:1-6, the elder John describes the method by which Jesus conquered. The essence of his method comes out in the contrast between how Jesus is described and how he appears. One of the elders surrounding the throne calls out to John: 'Look, the Lion of the tribe of Judah, the Root of David, has conquered!' (5:5, author's translation).

Expectant, John looks up, but he sees neither a lion nor a conqueror. Instead, in dramatic contrast, he records: 'Then I saw a Lamb, looking as if it had been slain' (5:6).

This is how the promised Messiah conquered: not through violence and military prowess, as many expected,[168] but through death, as a sacrificial victim. The Lion had come, but he came as a Lamb.

In this, Jesus serves as a model for the Christians of Asia Minor. He conquered through faithfulness to death; they must conquer in the same way.

The Church Conquers

The remainder of the vision portrays the suffering – and eventually the vindication – which awaits the church. Like Jesus, it is through suffering that the church conquers. All the same, it should be noted that he wins the decisive victory which defeats Satan. Christians merely win personal and corporate victories against the devil. As Leon Morris explains, 'Christians accordingly are not working towards victory, but from a victory already achieved.'[169]

In 6:10, the martyrs of God appear, slain because they had worshipped and witnessed to him. They cry out in a loud voice: 'How long, Sovereign Lord, holy and true, until you judge the inhabitants of the earth and avenge our blood?'

It should be noted that this is the only recorded prayer in Revelation (apart from praises offered to God). It is the opposite of warfare prayer. These people call out to God because they suffered at the hands of Satan, and in recognition that Satan retains power only so long as the sovereign God deigns to permit.

Somewhat surprisingly, the answer to their prayers is postponed: 'Each of them was given a white robe, and they were told to wait a little longer, until the number of their fellow-servants and brothers who were to be killed as they had been was completed' (6:11).

Just as the Lamb was slain (5:6), so must his people be (6:11). No special technique of prayer, traditional or innovative, is offered as the key to escaping persecution or defeating the demons.

To the contrary, just as the Lamb conquered through dying, so do his followers. Revelation 12 begins with Satan's attempt to destroy the Messiah; God intervenes, raising Jesus to heaven (12:4-5). Then war breaks out between Michael (with his angels) and Satan (with his demons). Satan loses, and is cast down from heaven to earth, along with his demons (12:7-9). Wagner cites Revelation 12 as 'a clear biblical account of strategic-level spiritual warfare.'[170] But, much like Daniel 10, this is warfare in heaven between angels and demons, not between man and the ruling spirits. In this battle, the angels fight without human help or prayer.[171] So if this is an example of SLSW, then humans are not to be involved.

Three consequences follow.[172] First, with the accuser of the brethren finally expelled from heaven, there is no longer any impediment to the salvation of the people of God:

> Now have come the salvation and the power and the kingdom
>   of our God, and the authority of his Christ,
> For the accuser of our brothers, who accuses them before
>   our God day and night, has been hurled down. (12:10)

Cast out from the presence of God, Satan is no longer able to argue for the condemnation of sinners (see Zech 3:1).

Secondly, despite the defeat of Satan, the church does not experience peace. In fact, because of his defeat, the situation becomes grim:

> Woe to the earth and the sea,
>   because the devil has gone down to you!
> He is filled with fury,
>   because he knows that his time is short. (12:12)

Like a wounded and cornered animal, Satan thrashes around desperately with the aim of injuring as many of his enemy as possible, before his own destruction. Christians are not called to overpower him: Christ and the angels have already done that. But they are warned not to take him for granted; he is both powerful and dangerous.[173]

Thirdly, Satan's efforts to destroy the Church give it the opportunity to conquer him:

> They conquered him through the blood of the lamb and through their
>   word of testimony.
> And they did not love their lives even to death.
> (Rev 12:11, author's translation)

Christians conquer Satan in the same way as Christ did: not through dramatic feats of power, but through faithful perseverance in suffering, even to the point of death (see also Rev 13:10; 14:12).

Ironically, then, as Satan conquers the people of God through killing them, he is in turn conquered by them. New Testament scholar Richard Bauckham states it well:

> The point is not that the beast and the Christians each win some victories; rather, the same event – the martyrdom of Christians – is described both as the beast's victory over them and as their victory over the beast.[174]

Yet, he adds, 'the martyrs are the real victors. To be faithful in witness to the true God even to the point of death is not to become a victim of the beast, but to take the field against him and win.'[175] The only way Christians can lose is 'to switch sides or to quit.'[176]

So the defeat of Satan does not mean the end of trouble for the church. To the contrary, it signals an escalation and intensification of opposition and persecution. But the end is in sight, and those who endure to the end shall be victorious, even if in the meantime they become victims. In the words of New Testament scholar Leon Morris:

> The evil one has been cast out of heaven. His power on earth is, to be sure, terrifyingly real to believers. But this is not because he is triumphant. It is because he knows that he is beaten and has but a short time. Let the church then take heart. She will have her martyrs, but ultimately triumph is sure.[177]

As the judgement of God begins on earth, John sees in heaven those who 'conquered' the beast (15:2). This victory was attained at great price, their own deaths (14:15). But it is worth the cost, for it is rewarded with a place in heaven (15:3-4).

Those who persist in faith through persecution and even death are not 'casualties of spiritual warfare' which can be reduced by careful implementation of powerful strategies.[178] They are conquering heroes, and are therefore accorded the highest honours and reward: they inherit heaven (Rev 15:2; 21:7). It is by becoming victims that they are victorious. It is in being conquered that they conquer.

The Final Conquest

The denouement in this lengthy drama brings the final downfall and imprisonment of Satan. The beast conspires with its allies to wage war against the Lamb. But despite apparent weakness, the Lamb is actually Lord over all lords and King over all kings. He 'conquers' the beast, and his followers share in the victory (17:1-14). Judgement is then

poured out on all who opposed Christ, and his martyred followers
finally see their vindication (18:1-21).

Hiebert comments on the similarity between Daniel and Revelation:

> As in Daniel, the divine warrior acts alone and the description of victory
> over the dragon reflects the author's confidence that ultimate powers
> were moving against repressive human institutions and would in the end
> reward the passive resistance of the faithful.[179]

The divine warrior is the sole active agent in the final battle; his followers are called merely to persevere in the midst of oppression.

There is one final, massive rebellion (20:1-9). But this is quickly
defeated, and the final judgement takes place. Those who opposed
God are sentenced to hell, along with Satan and his demons (20:10-
15).

Revelation ends with an extended portrait of the ethereal glories of
heaven (21:1-22:6). Recalling the exhortations to the churches of Asia
Minor, God promises: 'The one who conquers [*nikao*] will inherit these
things, and I will be his God and he will be my child' (21:7, author's
translation).

CONCLUSION

There is a great deal about Revelation which is unclear to modern
readers. But there can be no doubt about the present status of the war
against Satan, or the means by which Christians may conquer him.

The battle divides naturally into three stages. The first occurred at
the cross, and Satan was decisively and irrevocably defeated (Rev
12:1-9; cf. Eph 1:19-21; Col 2:15). As a result, he no longer stands
before God to obstruct the salvation of the people of God.

The second stage continues throughout the present. It is characterised by increased desperation and heightened aggression by the
powers of evil against the people of God (Rev 12:12-17).

The third phase awaits, when Christ shall return to imprison the
devil and his demons in hell for eternity, and to bring his people safely
home to heaven (Rev 20:1-15).

Those who dwell in this intervening period face a foe who is simultaneously defeated and destructive. Since he has already been defeated
by Christ, they need not take the offensive against him. But since he is
presently launching a counterattack, they must defend themselves.

In Revelation, Christians are called to beat back Satan's assaults, not to charge out against him. It is always he who attacks the church, not the reverse. A survey of the verb 'make war against' (*polemeo*) and the noun 'battle' (*polemos*) confirms this. The angels and demons battle each other in heaven (12:7). The kings of the world make war against Christ (17:14). Christ makes war against sinners (19:11-16). Satanic figures make war against Christians and Christ (12:17; 13:7; 16:14; 19:19; 20:8-9). But though these terms occur a total of fifteen times, not once do they describe Christians making war against Satan.

Revelation 13 makes it clear that this omission was intentional, not accidental:

> [People] worshipped the beast and asked, 'Who is like the beast? Who can make war against him?' (13:4)

This is a rhetorical question: it was obvious to them – though it is apparently not obvious to some Christians today – that no human could hope to make war against the beast. Certainly Christians cannot; instead, it is he who makes war against them.

> He [the beast] was given power to make war against the saints and to conquer them. (13:7)

The only recourse is to endure with patience, winning the victory through perseverance in the faith, even through martyrdom if necessary:

> If anyone is to go into captivity.
>   into captivity he will go,
> If anyone is to be killed with the sword,
>   with the sword he will be killed.
> This calls for patient endurance and faithfulness on the part of the
>   saints (13:10).[180]

Victory comes not by attacking, but by holding fast to the faith while under attack. In so doing, we, like Christ, conquer Satan.

The promise of more effective techniques for defeating the demonic horde slights the victory which Christ already has won for us. The belief that spirits can be rendered impotent in this age reflects impatience with God's timetable for binding Satan. The assertion that we can nullify the power of ruling spirits dishonours the millions of martyrs over the last two thousand years – and still others in our own time – who have honoured God faithfully in death. The suggestion that a short burst of a special kind of prayer can make all the difference in evangelism mocks those who plead with God for respite in the face of Satanic persecution, opposition and discouragement.

SLSW often promotes itself as seeing life 'as it really is, not as it seems to be'.[181] But with its emphasis on the power of Satan, the opposite is more the case. As George Ladd observes, 'The single intent of [Rev 12] is to assure those who meet satanic evil on earth that it is really a defeated power, however contrary it might seem to human experience.'[182]

Revelation agrees that life is not as it seems to be; but the discrepancy is just the opposite of what SLSW suggests. Life seems to be under the sway of the evil one. But in reality this is evidence of his defeat: 'The troubles of the persecuted righteous arise not because Satan is too strong, but because he is beaten. He is doing all the harm he can while he can. But he will not be able to do this for much longer.'[183]

CHAPTER FIVE

REPEATING THE MISTAKES OF HISTORY: SLSW IN THE INTERTESTAMENTAL PERIOD

Summary: Variations on SLSW were taught in intertestamental Jewish literature. The New Testament, however, implicitly rejects these teachings.

According to traditional wisdom, 'If something is new, it probably isn't true; and if something is true, it probably isn't new.' 'Tried and tested' was once a strong recommendation.

But times have changed. Now the cliché is: 'new and improved.' Innovation is taken to be inherently superior. History and tradition have only nostalgic value. 'State of the art' becomes not just an advertising slogan but an entire way of life.

This orientation carries over to theology and missions. Each change of season brings new fashions to Paris catwalks and new strategies in missions. Those who do not embrace the new are antediluvian in outlook, hopelessly out of touch with modern realities. So faced with criticism of SLSW, one proponent cites 'well-known social scientific laws of diffusion of innovation', to the effect that, 'any innovation typically draws early adopters, then middle adopters and finally late adopters. In many cases some refuse ever to adopt the innovation, as the existence of the International Flat Earth Society well demonstrates.... The knee-jerk Christian reaction when opposing any innovation is to say, 'It is not biblical.'[184]

Within the field of diffusion research, this attitude is known as 'pro-innovation bias': 'the implication ... that an innovation should be diffused and adopted by all members of a social system, that it should be diffused more rapidly, and that the innovation should be neither re-invented nor rejected.'[185] The bias overlooks the possibility of error, the consequent need for evaluation, and the modern tendency to embrace innovation for its prestige value.[186]

There was a time when tradition was a guide to truth. Now it is dismissed as an obstacle to progress. There was a time when historic orthodoxy was the chief test of spiritual wisdom. Now innovation is the leading measure of Spirit leading. Fascination with the advances of modern technology has crossed all reasonable boundaries into neophilia, a smug condescension toward the past and an uncritical fascination with anything new, in all fields.

In such an environment, little value attaches to the study of history. After all, if modern is superior, why bother with the ancients? The views of Augustine, Luther, Calvin or Wesley may be of quaint historical interest to those who are fascinated with antiquarian memorabilia, but they are hardly relevant in a modern age. So their place in personal libraries and in Christian bookstores has been taken over by newer and trendier authors.

In the case of spiritual warfare, there is irony in this disdain for history, because ideas similar to SLSW have appeared on at least two prior occasions: Jewish literature of the intertestamental period, and Christian literature in medieval times. This chapter surveys the intertestamental literature. The next considers medieval theology. In each case it is instructive to note both the source and the eventual fate of such teachings.

DEMONS IN INTERTESTAMENTAL LITERATURE

While demons are rare and obscure in the Old Testament, they come to the fore in the intertestamental period. Noted specialist D. S. Russell comments:

> When we enter the inter-testamental period we find that belief in angels has grown to proportions unknown in the Old Testament writings. Details of their numbers, their names, their functions, their natures are given which, though in many cases having their beginning in the canonical Scriptures, far outstrip anything to be found there.[187]

Surprisingly, though, this material is widely overlooked in current literature promoting SLSW. In a dozen books, I could find only a couple of references to a minor text from the Apocrypha, and nothing at all from the Pseudepigrapha.[188]

The Apocrypha and Pseudepigrapha are two collections of writings composed largely between 200 BC–AD 200. The Apocrypha includes fourteen writings of various genre, which were included in the ancient Greek translation of the Old Testament (the Septuagint) but excluded from the Hebrew Bible. Various branches of Christendom have taken different attitudes toward this literature. Roman Catholicism accepts the Apocrypha as 'deuterocanonical' (edifying but not fully authoritative); most Protestant denominations do not grant it any special status, though some would concede it a certain historical value.

The Pseudepigrapha is a less well-defined group of writings, varying somewhat in number according to the whim of the modern compiler. As the name implies, most were written under pseudonyms, usually the name of a respected biblical character, such as Adam, Abraham, Solomon, or Ezra, presumably in the hopes of gaining prestige and readership. They were generally written to reassure and inspire Jews suffering under foreign domination. Among the most pertinent for our purposes are the apocalyptic works, which recount the final triumph of

God over those who oppress his people.

No mainstream group, Jewish or Christian, has accorded the Pseudepigrapha canonical status. So this material is relevant not because it has special authority, but because it offers some striking parallels to SLSW.[189]

These writings do not endorse every tenet of SLSW; but they certainly provide much more support than does the Old Testament. The various works do not agree at every point and the material is vast, so this survey makes no effort to be comprehensive or systematic. Instead, it selects two texts which demonstrate the strongest affinities with SLSW.

THE DEMONS OF 1 ENOCH

Several intertestamental works reflect a fascination with the allusive story of sons of God intermarrying with the daughters of men and producing nephilim, the heroes of epic stories (Gen 6:1-4).[190] Like other works, 1 Enoch (2nd cent BC–1st cent AD) fills in the blanks left by Genesis. The brief biblical narrative becomes the basis for an expansive theology of fallen angels and demons (1 Enoch 6-15).

A Summary of the Story

It seems that these sons of God were licentious angels, two hundred in number, divided into companies of ten each, and led by one Semyaz. Knowing that they were acting sinfully, and fearful of punishment, they sought safety in numbers, banded together and left heaven to marry mortal women. The resultant offspring were giants who created havoc by their enormous appetites.

When the humans could no longer manage to produce enough food, the giants began eating them. The people cried out for relief. In response God sent the archangel Gabriel to stir the giants up to war against one another until they should all die. He also sent the archangel Michael to bind the fallen angels until the time of judgement when they would be cast into eternal torment.

But this was not the end of the problem: as the giants died, evil spirits came out of their bodies to dwell on the earth, where they promoted evil (ch 6-15). Toward the end of the book, when discussing the final judgement, 1 Enoch returns to these angels, called Watchers, to discuss their sins and their final destiny (ch 69).

1 Enoch and Territorial Spirits

Like SLSW, 1 Enoch endorses the concept of spirit hierarchies, but in a far more detailed version. Here the two hundred fallen angels are grouped into tens, fifties, and hundreds, with a chief at each level, and an overall leader (69:3; 6:3; 9:7). The devout angels are also bureaucratically arranged, but perhaps only in two levels: there are innumerable angels, with four, or perhaps seven, archangels (ch 20, 40). 1 Enoch makes no attempt to organise the evil spirits.

Unlike SLSW, though, the spirits are generally not geographical, but functional.[191] Each of the fallen angels teaches a different forbidden science to mankind: one teaches war, seduction and materialism; another teaches magical incantations; another, the breaking of incantations; another, astrology; another, the working of miracles; another, the interpretation of stars; and the list goes on (ch 8, 69).

The righteous angels also are functional: one has authority over the spirits of man; one takes revenge against the fallen angels and the evil spirits; one oversees the garden of Eden; one rules over the spirits of sinners; another is in charge of wounds and healing; yet another brings people to repentance (ch 10, 20, 40). One righteous angel oversees the peoples and nations of the earth, but his jurisdiction is universal, not territorial (20:5).

So while there is overlap between the demonic beliefs of 1 Enoch and the theory of territorial spirits, the divergence is greater than the correspondence. A review of warfare prayer reaches a similar conclusion.

1 Enoch and Warfare Prayer

Spirit names abound in 1 Enoch, as does prayer, but the two are not linked in the same way as in SLSW. In warfare prayer, the names are sought for use in cursing the demons. In 1 Enoch, the names serve no apparent purpose beyond satisfying curiosity.

According to 1 Enoch, the four leading archangels are Michael, Raphael, Gabriel and Phanuel. Other angels include: Asuryal, Suru'el, Raguel, Saraqa'el, Uriel, Ura'el and Rufael (ch 10, 20, 40). The names of the fallen angels are also given, and on two occasions. To be more precise, the entire two hundred are not named, but the leader of each group of ten is (though the lists are somewhat different). The overall leader is Semyaz; his immediate subordinates include Anan'el, Armaros, Dan'el, Tam'el and Zaqe'el, and some twenty others (ch 6, 69).

The author's purpose in giving these names is not entirely clear.

One point is evident, though: he never suggests that the names should be used in prayer to bind the demons. In fact, the demons do not need binding. Instead, facing judgement at the hands of God, the fallen spirits actually call on Enoch to request his intercession (ch 13-16). Notably, Enoch does not need any special information or technique to conquer the fallen angels. He is not at their mercy; they are at his.

Summary
SLSW and 1 Enoch agree at least in part on two points: spirits are arranged in hierarchies and have proper names.

At three other points, 1 Enoch differs from SLSW. As noted, 1 Enoch offers no hint of territoriality, no suggestion that people gain some advantage from using the name of the spirits, nor any indication that one sort of prayer is more effective than others.

For its part, SLSW would presumably dispute a couple of points from 1 Enoch, including the idea that evil spirits issue from the giant offspring of angels who cohabited with humans, or the idea that the planets and stars are heavenly spirits (whose names, ranks and functions should also be determined).

So 1 Enoch cannot provide much support for SLSW. Essentially, the two systems merely share a strong interest in evil spirits, and a willingness to speculate about what Scripture does not reveal. At times their conjectures converge, but these occasions appear to be random coincidences. All the same, 1 Enoch shares a basic orientation with SLSW which the Old Testament does not.

DEFEATING DEMONS IN THE TESTAMENT OF SOLOMON
While a survey of demonology and angelology in the intertestamental literature could continue at great length, perhaps only one more source provides sufficient parallels to warrant attention here.[192] The Testament of Solomon combines a narrative of the building of the temple with Solomon's reputation for powers of healing and exorcism.[193] The story-line provides extensive information about demons, and models a method for controlling them.[194]

A Summary of the Story
A boy working on the temple is preyed upon by a demon who steals half his pay and provisions. As the boy grows ever thinner, Solomon begs God for authority over the demon. In response, the archangel

Michael brings a ring which enables Solomon to bind all demons and to conscript them into his service (1:1-7).

When the demon next appears, the boy uses the ring to capture it and then brings it to the king. With an oath, Solomon forces the demon to tell the truth. By interrogating the demon, he discovers its name, function, place of residence in the heavens, as well as the name of the angel who can defeat it.[195] He then sets the demon to work on the temple (1:8-2:8).

This works so well that Solomon gives the ring to the first demon and forces him to bring Beelzeboul, the prince of the demons. Beelzeboul then serves as an informant, introducing other demons one by one. Once Solomon identifies their functions, places of residence, and opposing angels, he constricts their powers and assigns them to build the temple. Whenever one resists, he appeals to the opposing angel for help or invokes the name of the angel in an oath (ch 3-25).

Once again, the evidence for SLSW is mixed. As with 1 Enoch, there is more support for the practice of warfare prayer than for the theory of territorial spirits. Yet also as before, the dissimilarities outnumber the similarities.

The Testament of Solomon and Territorial Spirits

The Testament makes no distinction between strategic-level spirits and ground-level spirits. Instead, the evil spirits are simultaneously heavenly and earthly: they dwell in the various signs of the zodiac, yet they afflict people on earth (2:2).

There are hints of a spirit hierarchy, but it consists of only two tiers: angels and archangels; demons and the prince of demons. Among the archangels are Michael (1:6) and Ouriel (2:7). Beelzeboul is the prince of demons (3:1-6), and was formerly the highest ranking angel in heaven (6:2).

Finally, the demons are functional rather than territorial. Some spirits promote sin, others cause natural disasters; yet others bring illness, physical deformity or death. The list is seemingly endless: spirits of murder and war, of wind and fire, of deception and heresy, of strife and grave-robbing, of birth defects and still births, of tonsillitis and flatulence. Every imaginable problem faced on earth may be traced back to the malicious machinations of the demonic horde.

So the theory of territorial spirits finds little support here. But the Testament gives a fair bit of attention to overcoming the evil machinations of demons, so it may still support the practice of warfare prayer.

The Testament of Solomon and Prayer

The Testament is a mine of information for those committed to naming the spirits. It also supports the assumption that knowing the name of a spirit conveys power over it.

Dozens of spirit names appear. The spirit who attacks newlyweds is Asmodeus. The spirit of sea storms is Kunopegos. The spirit of headaches is Barsafael. The spirit of domestic violence, Katanikotael. The spirit of divorce, Modebel. The spirit of haemorrhoids, Rhyx Axesbuth. The spirit who causes people to swallow fish bones, Rhyx Aleureth. More than a hundred righteous angels and evil spirits appear here, and only a very few lack names.

Virtually whatever the problem, the Testament of Solomon provides the name of the demon who causes it. But there is a notable difference between the Testament and SLSW at this point. SLSW often seeks the names of the spirits through prayer, historical research and personal revelation. The Testament provides the names so that there is no need for prayer, revelation or research.

The Testament also uses the power of names to control the spirits, but again not in the same way as SLSW. It is not the name of the demon which gives Solomon power over them. Rather, when a demon resists, Solomon calls for the assistance of the corresponding angel who subdues the demon. In this case, warfare prayer is not bold confrontation with demons which renders them impotent. It is a confession of human impotence and a cry for angelic intervention.

Summary

In brief, the Testament of Solomon finds some agreement with SLSW at two points. Both name the spirits and both use the names in warfare prayer.

Even here, though, there are significant differences. The Testament of Solomon provides the relevant names instead of urging its readers to seek them in prayer.[196] The Testament provides many more specific, proper names, while SLSW often resorts to generic descriptions. The Testament names not only the demons, but also the angels. Which all goes to say, that if God is truly calling the church to engage in warfare prayer, the Testament of Solomon provides far more detailed information and concrete help than any of the recent books promoting SLSW.

At the same time, the use of the Testament would require some modifications in the practice of warfare prayer. SLSW uses the names of the demons in prayer; the Testament uses the names of the angels.[197] In SLSW, warfare prayer is the means by which believers gain control of the spirits. According to the Testament, prayer is the means by which those who fail to gain control over the spirits can appeal to a superior being to wage war on their behalf.

The use of the Testament would also require the endorsement of beliefs which many people today might be reluctant to affirm. Apart from the question of praying to angels, at least some proponents of SLSW would balk at the suggestion that such illnesses as colic, flu, insomnia, and swallowing fish bones are demon-induced. Do the demons dwell in the sky, in the locations of the zodiac signs? Should we obtain the liver and gall of the sheatfish to use in exorcism (5:9,13)? Can crib deaths be prevented by writing out a charm invoking the angel Raphael against the demon Obyzouth (13:3-6)? Can we, like Solomon, use demons to construct our church buildings?

CONCLUSION

In the intertestamental literature for the first time we find considerable support for SLSW. Not for all its tenets, perhaps, but at least for some. Clearly around the time of the first century, some Jews believed demons to be arranged in one sort of bureaucracy or another, and to be vulnerable to those who know their names.

At the same time, some of the related teachings in the intertestamental literature are sure to raise eyebrows. Anyone who cites these texts in support of SLSW (or any other theory) must address the awkward teachings, not quietly side-step them.

So for those who practise SLSW, the evaluation of this literature is not a simple matter. It is clearly easier to ignore it: this would side-step considerable conflicting data, and the encumbrance of the bizarre teachings. Yet that means losing the best support uncovered thus far.

Moreover, this material may not simply be ignored. It is non-canonical, and thus non-authoritative, but the same could be said of contemporary writings endorsing SLSW. We are faced with several competing concepts of spiritual warfare from the intertestamental literature, with several more variations coming from proponents of

SLSW. The crucial question, then, is: If we feel the need to go beyond the explicit teachings of Scripture, which approach to spiritual warfare should we endorse? Which theory is correct? Which practice is effective? Or if none is entirely correct, how do we determine which parts are accurate, and which erroneous?

But the most pressing and difficult problem of all is posed by the New Testament data, when read in the light of intertestamental theory and practice. Clinton Arnold, author of two scholarly works on demons in the New Testament, identifies six points at which the apostle Paul is silent, in contrast to the Jewish literature of the time:

(1) Paul does not discuss the origin of the demons;
(2) Paul does not reconstruct spirit hierarchies;
(3) Paul does not affirm territorial jurisdiction;
(4) Paul does not name the powers;
(5) Paul does not list the functions of various spirits;
(6) Paul does not teach techniques for thwarting demons.[198 and 199]

Strikingly, at each point where Paul is silent, SLSW speaks. In short, SLSW has more in common with intertestamental Judaism than with New Testament Christianity.[200]

CHAPTER SIX

LEARNING FROM THE PAST: SLSW IN CHURCH HISTORY

Summary: Many early and medieval Church Fathers reconstructed demon taxonomies, but even at their wildest, they did not come close to the magnitude of present speculations. Even so, their theories were roundly condemned by the Reformers.

The closest parallels to SLSW undoubtedly come from intertestamental Judaism and from ancient magic. Both, like SLSW, view man as the victim of capricious spirits. Both, again like SLSW, affirm that those who name the spirits gain power over them. In addition, various intertestamental writings rank the spirits in hierarchies and allot them specialised functions (albeit not geographical territories).

Such close parallels apparently never recur in the history of Christianity, but at various times more limited affinities with SLSW have appeared. In particular, the early and the medieval church considered four of the tenets promoted by SLSW: spirit territories, names, and hierarchies, as well as prayer marches. A survey of these teachings, and the Reformers' response to them, provides insight into the present discussion.

It bears repeating that to be relevant, the historical evidence must pertain to the distinctives of SLSW. Most of the supporting material cited by proponents concerns exorcism.[201] But according to the taxonomy of SLSW, spirits which possess people are a different class of demon from territorial spirits, so this material is irrelevant. Fortunately, a fair bit of relevant evidence does appear in church history, though it largely undermines, rather than supports, SLSW.

SLSW & THE EARLY AND MEDIEVAL CHURCH

After the New Testament era, demons are not forgotten. Numerous apostolic Fathers discuss them at length.[202] Since the works are vast, diverse, and often untranslated, the teachings are not easily surveyed.[203] So this section is illustrative, and makes no pretence to being comprehensive. But for all that, certain trends are readily apparent.

Territorial Spirits

Currently the concept of demonic territories is built on the narrow foundation of two texts, Deuteronomy 32:8 and Daniel 10:13,20. Interestingly enough, these verses were also known to the Church Fathers, though they did not attempt to construct such a vast edifice upon them.

On the basis of the Daniel text, Theodoret of Cyr (393-466) concludes that all nations have guardian angels.[204] Pseudo-Dionysius (c. 500) concurs, though he is careful to avoid the idea that God is just another local deity, ruling over Israel while other gods govern the rest of the world. Rather, God is sovereign over all nations, and does not share his authority with the angels, though he does appoint Michael to oversee Israel, and more angels to supervise the other nations.[205]

Other Fathers extend this principle to regions and cities. According to John Damascene (645-749), angels guard the regions of the earth, including both nations and places, assisting man and managing his affairs.[206]

To this, Hiliary of Poitiers (315-367) adds, based on Revelation 2-3, that each church has a guardian angel.[207] The concept of guardian spirits over individuals is also widely accepted in the early and medieval church.[208]

In short, nations, cities, churches, peoples and individuals are all widely believed to have guardian spirits. But are these territorial demons? Quite clearly not.

For one reason, they may not even be demons. In discussing Daniel 10:13, Aquinas cites both Jerome and Gregory to explain that the 'prince' of Persia was a good angel, seeking the welfare of Israel, not an evil spirit opposed to it.[209]

For another, they are not specifically geographical. Those most similar to territorial spirits are consistently assigned to nations, not to the geographical areas, and would better be considered 'geopolitical' spirits. The concept of territoriality also makes little sense in the case of guardian angels over churches, peoples or individuals.[210]

Confirming the view that guardian spirits are not territorial, Aquinas defends the concept that every visible object has an angelic guardian. With Origen, he postulates that every beast, tree, plant, and every corporeal object has a guardian spirit. These spirits do not take up residence in the object; neither do they preside over the region where the object is located. Rather, they preside over the object itself.[211] They are ecological and custodial spirits; they are not territorial.

Tertullian (155-240) explicitly excludes the idea that angels are restricted to particular geographical regions. Both angels and demons, he observed, are winged: 'Therefore they are everywhere in a moment. The whole world is but one place to them.'[212] Similarly, in describing the guardian spirits over individuals, Aquinas insists that they are always on the job. When they are in heaven they guard a man and can return to him instantly, if necessary.[213] The angels do not live with their client; they move about freely, while always watching out for him.

Another contrast between the theology of the Fathers and the proposals of SLSW is noteworthy. In SLSW, the territorial spirits constitute the highest level of the hierarchy, 'strategic-level' spirits. In the Church Fathers, on the other hand, guardian spirits come from the lowest levels.[214]

Probably the closest equivalent to territorial spirits comes in populist medieval beliefs about saints. In his study of magic in pre-Reformation England, Keith Thomas notes that

> Individual churches had their own patron saints, and strong territorial associations could give hagiolatry an almost totemic character: 'Of all Our Ladies,' says a character in one of Thomas More's writings, 'I love best Our Lady of Walsingham', 'and I', saith the other, 'Our Lady of Ipswich.'[215]

At the same time, each trade had its own saint, as did the various diseases. Every part of their lives were thought to be under the protection of different saints: their towns, occupations, families, churches, and so forth.[216]

But even this is different in several respects from the concept of territorial spirits. The saints are benevolent, spiritualised humans, not malevolent demons. Their jurisdictions are not distinctly geographical but multifarious. This belief is also part of a larger system which Thomas characterises as magical,[217] subsequently vehemently opposed by the Reformers.[218]

Warfare Prayer

The major practices of warfare prayer were also known in the early and medieval periods, though they were rejected – rather than practised – by Christians.

From time to time a Father does identify a spirit by name, but never with the purpose that proponents of SLSW have in mind. Origen, for example, lists the names of three, but only three angels, and he finds them not through direct revelation or through demon interrogation, but in the intertestamental literature.[219] Justin Martyr simplifies the process, by accepting the names assigned by pagans to their gods.[220] By this logic, it is a simple matter to identify the names of the demons around today: we simply interview their worshippers.

A major reason why the Fathers give little thought to demon names is simply that such knowledge served no useful function. These writings give no example of anyone invoking the name of the demons in warfare prayer: to the contrary, that is explicitly shunned as pagan sorcery!

Celsus accused Christians of practising magic: after all, they invoke a powerful name to cast out demons. In reply, Origen draws an important distinction between Christian exorcism and pagan rituals. The Christians do nothing more, he says, than to call on the name of Jesus and read passages of Scripture. Magicians, on the other hand, use incantations and invoke all manner of powerful names.[221]

Similarly, Augustine explains how Christians conquer Satan, and it has nothing to do with knowing the names of the demons:

> It is by true piety that men of God cast out the hostile power of the air which opposes godliness; it is by exorcising it, not by propitiating it; and they overcome all the temptations of the adversary by praying, not to him, but to their own God against him.[222]

For this kind of prayer, he insists, the only necessary name is that of Jesus.

The differences between historic Christianity and SLSW are just as evident when it comes to the results expected from spiritual warfare. None of the Fathers anticipates that spiritual warfare would ensure an end to persecution, let alone success in evangelism.

To those facing persecution, Origen counsels perseverance. He warns that those who recant under pressure submit once again to demonic authority, while the death of martyrs marks their victory over the devil.[223] He insists that man has nothing to fear from the demons, because God protects him, whether directly or through the agency of guardian angels.[224] The only time demons can defeat Christians is if the Christians let them; all they need do is to pray to God and to use the provisions outlined by Paul in Ephesians 6:11-12.[225]

Similarly, arguing against those who say that the world is under the sway of Satan, Chrysostom responds that if this were so, we would all be in the same condition as the demoniac of Mark 5.[226] Both he and Augustine insist that neither Satan nor demons can do anything without divine permission. Even persecution against the church is subject to the sovereignty of God, who uses it for good in the lives of his people.[227]

Spirit Hierarchies

The closest agreement between the medieval church and practitioners of SLSW comes in the construction of spirit taxonomies. In the end, their results do not agree either among themselves or with their modern counterparts. But at least both the ancients and SLSW engage in a similar practice.

The most popular medieval scheme divided the spirits into nine categories, arranged in three groups of three. Pseudo-Dionysius is generally credited with this innovation, though he attributes it to his teacher, Hierotheus.[228] In any event, while this basic structure proved popular, consensus was never reached on either the labels or their order. A representative sample illustrates the divergence:

1) seraphim, cherubim, thrones; dominations, virtues, powers; principalities, archangels, angels (Pseudo-Dionysius, John Damascene);[229]

2) seraphim, cherubim, thrones; dominations, principalities, powers; virtues, archangels, angels (Gregory the Great);[230]

3) seraphim, cherubim, thrones; powers, principalities, dominations; virtues, archangels, angels (Cyril of Jerusalem);[231]

4) virtues, ascents, splendours; powers, principalities, dominations; thrones, archangels, angels (Gregory of Nazianz);[232]

5) dominations, thrones, virtues, powers, principalities (Basil the Great);[233]

6) dominations, powers, principalities, archangel, angel (Jerome);[234]

7) thrones, dominations, principalities, powers (Augustine).[235]

Undoubtedly the most dramatic example of variation comes in the writings of John Chrysostom (344-407). He provides at least six lists, no two of which are the same![236]

These variations call the entire enterprise into question. In fact, this point is widely conceded by ancient writers, even by some of those who attempt it. Gregory of Nazianz concludes his list by remarking, 'You see how this reasoning dizzies us, and we can make no progress in it.'[237] Similarly, Augustine comments, 'Let those who are able answer these questions, if they can also prove their answers to be true; but as for me, I confess my ignorance.'[238] Perhaps this would still be the wiser counsel.

Spirit Corporeality
The rationale for territorial spirits is also reminiscent of medieval debates.

> Satan is getting away with a lot. But how does he do it? How does he blind 3 billion or more minds?
>
> Obviously, Satan cannot do it by himself. Satan is not God, nor does he possess any of the attributes of God. This means among other things

that Satan is not omnipresent. He cannot be in all places at all times as God is. Satan can be in only one place at one time. He may be able to get from one place to another very rapidly, but when he is there, he is still in only one place.

The only way I can imagine that Satan can effectively blind 3 billion minds is to delegate the responsibility. He maintains a hierarchy of demonic forces to carry out his purposes.[239]

Contrary to popular perception, there is no evidence to suggest that the medieval Fathers debated how many angels could dance on the head of a pin. But they did debate a related issue, one touched on in the preceding quote: spirit corporeality.

Do angels and demons have bodies? If so, what sort of substance are they made of? How do they move from place to place? The gist of the debate focused on one question: When angels or demons move from one place to another, must they pass through any intervening regions (or might they, like the crew of the 'Starship Enterprise', merely 'beam' from one location directly to the next)?

Aquinas did not start the debate, but he offered his contribution in five propositions. First, he agrees that spirits can be in only one place at a time. Secondly, because they are spirit, they are not in a place in the same sense that a human being would be.

For a body is in a place in a circumscribed fashion, since it is measured by the place. An angel, however, is not there in a circumscribed fashion, since he is not measured by the place, but definitively, because he is in one place in such a manner that he is not in another. But God is neither circumscriptively nor definitively there, because he is everywhere.[240]

Thirdly, spirits can move from one place to another, but in a different sense than humans do. For an angel to be 'in' a place means nothing more than that it exercises its power toward that place. Consequently, in 'moving' from one place to another, the spirit merely shifts the focus of its attention. Fourthly, in so 'moving', it may or may not pass through intermediate space, depending on whether the movement is continuous or not. Finally, spirits do not move instantaneously.[241]

Much could, of course, be said about either analysis, but for present purposes it suffices to note that both SLSW and the medieval Fathers are asking the same sort of questions. What is the nature of spirit presence? Both are agreed that spirits have no bodies but are nonetheless localised in their activity. Where they differ, however, is in

SLSW's assumption that spirits maintain a fixed residence, while the Fathers assume them to be mobile. It is marvellous what speculative theology can do with a little spare time and a creative imagination![242]

Prayer Marches

In a final affinity with SLSW, the later medieval church conducted regular prayer marches. On the day of Rogations, priests would lead processions around the borders of the fields, carrying a cross, banners and bells, in order to drive away evil spirits and to ensure high crop yields. The Reformers condemned such beliefs and practices as magic, arguing that prayer was just as effective if uttered inside the walls of a church as outside in the fields.[243]

Summary

In his latest work promoting SLSW, Wagner summarises his historical method in five principles:

(1) *"Not everything that happens is recorded."*
(2) *"Not everything written has been preserved."*
(3) *"Not everything preserved has been found."*
(4) *"Not everything found is available."*
(5) *"Not everything available is interpreted in the same way."*[244]

On these grounds, he concludes, whether history provides no clear examples of SLSW, or a few, or even a great many, 'does not matter much.... In any of the three cases it is still possible to justify the validity of strategic-level spiritual warfare, keeping in mind the five principles.'[245]

This is an extraordinary methodology. If history provides the desired data, all well and good. If history proves silent, then the hoped-for events can nonetheless be inferred on the assumption that the reports were either not recorded, preserved, rediscovered, circulated, or properly interpreted. By this rationale, historical research is pointless.

But at least one of his five principles is unwittingly established in the way he uses the evidence he cites: 'Not everything available is interpreted in the same way.' From his survey of early church history, Ramsay MacMullen argues that of all the motivations which prompted conversions to Christianity in early centuries, its perceived power over demons was primary. This is an obvious endorsement of SLSW, according to Wagner, 'as any reader of MacMullen's work will immediately see.'[246] In point of fact, however, MacMullen refers only to 'the expulsion of supernatural beings from diseased persons or from their dwellings in altars and statues' (i.e., to exorcism and to the cleansing of temples).[247]

Similarly, Wagner cites numerous specific examples from MacMullen, including Church Fathers Justin, Irenaeus, Tertullian and Cyprian, and concludes:

> My hope is that when [an unnamed critic] reads this chapter he will decide to modify his statement that he must reject strategic-level spiritual warfare because he has not found it illustrated in the history of the Christian Church.[248]

His hope is unlikely to be realised, at least not on the basis of the evidence cited. Every one of these examples refers to the exorcism of demons from people, idols or temples. Not a single one refers to territorial spirits. The same is true of every other example which MacMullen provides.

While methodology is thus a concern, closer examination of the historical data suggests that ultimately the explicit affirmations and denials of history are more problematic than its silences.

According to the early and medieval Fathers, custodial spirits are not geographical, nor are they high-ranking; they may not even be demons. The use of names in prayer directed at demons is what characterises pagan magic and distinguishes it from Christian practice. The Christian is called to remain faithful through opposition to the gospel, not promised a special technique for overwhelming the opposition. The Fathers acknowledge the reality, power and malice of demons, yet entrust themselves to the sovereignty of God, the victory of Christ, the protection of guardian angels, and the purity of holy living.

The only aspect of SLSW which the medieval church supports is the attempt to reconstruct spirit hierarchies. Even here, the similarity is only partial. None of the various reconstructions matches SLSW. Many Fathers despaired of reaching reliable conclusions. And they were generally concerned with angelic, rather than demonic, hierarchies.

Finally, the reluctance of the Fathers to invent new doctrines is worth noting. Origen is a striking example. Though known for extravagant interpretations of Scripture, even he draws clear limits to speculation. In developing his doctrine of demons, he writes:

> But that we may not appear to build our assertions on subjects of such importance and difficulty on the ground of inference alone, or to require the assent of our hearers to what is only conjectural, let us see whether we can obtain any declarations from holy Scripture, by the authority of which these positions may be more credibly maintained.[249]

While medieval exegesis as a whole is hardly cautious, the Fathers at least attempt to avoid unbridled speculation.

Many of the Fathers were fascinated with spirits and were familiar with all the relevant biblical texts. They were also willing to resort to considerable speculation in an effort to fill in the blanks left in Scripture. Nonetheless, they did not come up with the concept of territorial spirits, or with the practice of warfare prayer. If nothing else, their example makes it clear that SLSW is neither a necessary, nor even a natural, inference from Scripture.

SLSW & THE REFORMERS

As one might expect, the Reformers have even less patience with speculation about demons. According to some recent populist reappraisals of Church history, their reluctance is driven not by fidelity to Scripture but by conformity to Enlightenment rationalism. This is worse than caricature; it is drivel. The Reformers did indeed react against medieval speculation. But at the same time, they retained a high sensitivity to the demonic world.

This survey focuses on three figures, Luther, Calvin, and Wesley, for the simple reasons that they are three of the most prominent leaders in the Reformation and post-Reformation periods and their writings are readily available.

Martin Luther (1483-1546)

Luther makes no attempt to disguise his disdain for the speculative theology of the medieval church, Pseudo-Dionysius and his angelic hierarchies in particular.

> I would ask, by what authority and with what arguments does he prove his hodgepodge about the angels in his *Celestial Hierarchy* – a book over which many curious and superstitious spirits have cudgelled their brains? If one were to read and judge without prejudice, is not everything in it his own fancy and very much like a dream?[250]

Speculative theology, he insists, belongs in hell.[251] Conjecture about matters unknowable does not demonstrate profound spiritual insight; rather, it succumbs to Satanic temptation.

> A man must as vehemently strive against such cogitations as against unbelief, despair, heresies, and such like temptations. For most of us are deceived herewith, not believing they proceed from the devil, who yet himself fell through those very cogitations.[252]

All such questions he dismisses out of hand.

> When one asked, where God was before heaven was created? .... I said: He was building hell for such idle, presumptuous, fluttering and inquisitive spirits as you.[253]

If God has not revealed the truth of the matter explicitly in Scripture, we are better off leaving it alone.

But let it be stated clearly: this does not reflect rationalistic disbelief in the spirit world. Luther has a very vivid experience of demons: 'Almost every night when I wake up the devil is there and wants to dispute with me.'[254] Similarly, he notes, 'the devil looks for me when I am at home in bed, and one or two devils constantly lie in wait for me.'[255] So while he speculates less than his medieval predecessors, Lutheran scholar Paul Althaus can say, 'Luther takes the devil much more seriously than the Middle Ages did.'[256]

The devil is a fearsome and deceitful opponent, Luther warns:

> In short, the devil is too clever and too mighty for us. He resists and hinders us at every point.... Choose, then, whether you prefer to wrestle with the devil or whether you prefer to belong to him. If you consent to be his, you will receive his guarantee to leave you in peace with the Scriptures. If you refuse to be his, defend yourself, go at him! He will not pass you by.[257]

One could hardly ask for a more forceful call to spiritual warfare than this.

How then do we cope with such a fearsome opponent? Luther counsels confidence: Christians need not fear the devil, and for two reasons. First of all, God is sovereign over him. Satan cannot do anything without divine permission, and he can do nothing that does not in some way further God's aims.[258] Secondly, Christ has defeated him on the cross. Consequently, in Christ, 'sin, death, the wrath of God, hell, the devil, and all evils [are] conquered and put to death.'[259]

Turning to the specifics of SLSW, two features stand out in Luther's recommendations. The first is simplicity. 'Don't get too daring,' he warns; 'Satan has had thousands of years of practice and we do not know a hundredth part of what he knows.'[260] So, for example, when consulted by a pastor who complains of ghosts making a racket in his house at night, he counsels prayer to God and a simple rebuke: 'Be off, Satan! I am lord in this house, not you.'[261]

The second notable feature of his battle strategy is the weapons of war. There is nothing here about seeking the names of demons through divine revelation, nor anything about special techniques designed to make prayer powerful. Instead, he urges reliance upon Scripture and sacrament, and especially the former.

> God provided his church with audible preaching and visible sacraments. Satan resists this holy ministry in all earnestness, and he would like it to be eliminated altogether because by it alone is Satan overcome. The power of the oral Word is truly remarkable. To think that Satan, that proud spirit, may be put to flight and thrown into confusion by such a frail word on human lips![262]

The preaching of Scripture 'produces and strengthens faith, conquers sin, the devil, death, hell, and all evil.'[263] Had Eve only clung to the word of God, she could have resisted the temptation of the serpent. Letting go the word, she fell into sin. This is a universal principle: 'When one lets the Word go, there can be no other result.'[264] This emphasis upon the truth of God revealed in Scripture is the main reason why he rejects medieval speculation concerning demons, on the one hand, and the claims to new revelation by extremists in his own time, on the other.[265]

It is clear that Luther would have rejected SLSW had it been taught in his day. He explicitly rejected the closest contemporary parallel, the teaching of Pseudo-Dionysius, whose beliefs and practices were considerably more moderate than SLSW. Of course, this does not prove that SLSW is wrong. We cannot automatically assume that Luther is correct. But his rejection of speculative demonology and his reservations concerning new teachings should at least prompt caution in those who would claim to be his spiritual descendants.

John Calvin (1509-1564)

When it comes to theological speculation, Calvin shares the same perspective as Luther.

> Let us here remember that on the whole subject of religion one rule of modesty and soberness is to be observed, and it is this, – in obscure matters not to speak or think, or even long to know, more than the Word of God has delivered. A second rule is, that in reading the Scriptures we should constantly direct our inquiries and meditations to those things which tend to edification, not indulge in curiosity, or in studying things of no use.[266]

But he is not content to leave the matter in such general terms. Rather, like Luther also, he explicitly singles out issues such as angelic – or demonic – hierarchies and the views of Pseudo-Dionysius in particular.

> If we would be duly wise, we must renounce those vain babblings of idle men, concerning the nature, ranks, and numbers of angels, without any authority from the Word of God. I know that many fasten on these topics more eagerly, and take greater pleasure in them than in those relating to daily practice.... None can deny that Dionysius ... has many shrewd and subtle disquisitions in his *Celestial Hierarchy*; but on looking at them more closely, every one must see that they are merely idle talk. The duty of a theologian, however, is not to tickle the ear, but confirm the conscience, by teaching what is true, certain, and useful.[267]

So for Calvin, no less than for Luther, Scripture provides all that is needed for spiritual warfare. Pursuit of other details not covered in the Bible is not merely worthless but harmful.

Calvin also speaks to the issue of territoriality. Based on Daniel 10, he infers that certain angels (not demons) are appointed as rulers over nations and provinces. But he understands them to be guardian, not territorial.[268]

With respect to naming angels and constructing angelic hierarchies, he notes that Scripture offers only two names (Michael and Gabriel) and two levels (angel and archangel). He is unwilling to go beyond this.

> Farther than this, in regard both to the ranks and numbers of angels, let us class [such questions] among those mysterious subjects, the full revelation of which is deferred to the last day, and accordingly refrain from inquiring too curiously, or talking presumptuously.[269]

In his view, speculation is not a mark of spiritual insight; it is a mark of carnal presumption.

When it comes to spiritual warfare, Calvin also agrees with Luther that God is sovereign over the devil, so that ultimately and fundamentally we trust God rather than fearing Satan. Though Satan is opposed to God and to the people of God, the examples of Job, Ahab and Saul demonstrate that he can do only what God permits: 'As God holds him bound and fettered by the curb of his power, he executes those things only for which permission has been given him, and thus, however unwilling, obeys his Creator.'[270]

This does not mean that Satan poses no threat to the Christian, or that we can afford to take him for granted. Indeed, insists Calvin, all of Scripture's teaching about the devil has one aim, to put us on our guard.

> Being forewarned of the constant presence of an enemy the most daring, the most powerful, the most crafty, the most indefatigable, the most completely equipped with all the engines, and the most expert in the science of war, let us not allow ourselves to be overtaken by sloth or cowardice, but, on the contrary, with minds aroused and ever on the alert, let us stand ready to resist; and, knowing that this warfare is terminated only by death, let us study to persevere. Above all, fully conscious of our weakness and want of skill, let us invoke the help of God, and attempt nothing without trusting in him, since it is his alone to supply counsel, and strength, and courage, and arms.[271]

So we must constantly be on our guard against Satan.[272]

This we do by using the armour of Ephesians 6:11-17. Chief among these weapons are the shield and sword, that is, faith and the Word of God.

> By faith we repel all the attacks of the devil, and by the Word of God the enemy himself is slain outright. In other words, if the Word of God shall be efficacious in us through faith, we shall be more than sufficiently armed both for repelling and for putting to flight the enemy.[273]

We fight the demons also through prayer, but this is not aggressive warfare prayer which challenges the demons; it is calling upon God. In Calvin's theology there is neither place for, nor need of, any special technique for conquering the demons. God provides all we need in Scripture, prayer and faith.

Scripture does not tell us any more than this about the demonic world for the simple reason that we need not know. 'The Holy Spirit,' Calvin insists, 'could not deign to feed curiosity with idle, unprofitable histories. We see it was the Lord's purpose to deliver nothing in his sacred oracles which we might not learn for edification.' 'Therefore,' he exhorts, 'instead of dwelling on superfluous matters, let it be sufficient for us.'[274]

John Wesley (1703-1791)

Though his ministry took place some time after the Reformation, Wesley's views are worth considering because of his influence in the Church through the Methodist movement, and also because of his openness to manifestations of supernatural power.

Despite this openness, Wesley had no more patience with speculations about the demons than did Luther or Calvin. Like them, he insisted on restricting beliefs to what has been revealed in Scripture.

> Of angels, indeed, we know nothing with any certainty but by revelation; the accounts which are left by the wisest of the ancients, or given by the modern Heathens, being no better than silly, self-inconsistent fables, too gross to be imposed even upon children.[275]

He was unwilling to trust either the Church Fathers or modern animists; like the Reformers, Scripture alone was his authority.

This obviously limits the teachings which he shares in common with SLSW. He restricts the demonic hierarchy to two levels: Satan and the horde of demons. He allows that demons are 'governors of the world' (Eph. 6:12), but never takes this in a geographical sense. He agrees that demons are constantly warring against man in general and Christians in particular. But in the absence of explicit Scriptural teaching, he is unwilling to affirm the speculations characteristic of the medieval period.[276]

When Wesley counsels Christians how to overcome the devil, two emphases stand out. For one, he repeatedly insists that Satan is subject to the sovereignty of God. Demons actively and aggressively seek to corrupt man, but only 'as far as God is pleased to permit.'[277] Demons rule the world, 'so far as God permits!'[278] Thus while Satan wars constantly against us, looking for every opportunity to tempt us into sin and away from God,[279] a more fundamental truth is that we are under the guiding and protecting hand of God. Our focus is thus to be on the

God who reigns rather than on the demons who oppose us.

For the other, Christians defend themselves against Satan's attacks by means of the weapons which God provides and which the Bible describes. When Satan draws attention to our sin, we rejoice in the biblical promise that one day sin will be done away with. When he attacks our peace, we turn to Christ, who justifies through faith. When he attacks our faith, we cling on to that which we have thus far attained. We praise God for what he has done thus far in our lives, and strive for holiness.[280]

Which is to say, we do not seek additional techniques guaranteed to bring us victory. Rather, we persevere in the Christian disciplines revealed in Scripture. We pursue godliness; we hold fast to the faith; we cling to the promises of God. We do not attack the evil one; it is he who attacks us. In defence, we do not counterattack; instead, we turn to God, who is sovereign over Satan; and to Christ, who has defeated him.

CONCLUSION

Considering the numerous theological differences between the founding fathers of Protestantism, their agreement on spiritual warfare is striking. Each explicitly rejects much of the medieval teaching about the demons. They insist on a return to Scripture and renounce later accretions and extravagant speculations. In no way does this represent the triumph of rationalism over a belief in the supernatural. The Reformers' opposition to such teaching and practices does not spring from a disbelief in demons. It springs from belief in the Bible.

This is in fact one of the most prominent features of early Protestantism: *sola Scriptura*, Scripture alone. And it is meant in two senses: Scripture provides the content of our faith; and, Scripture provides all that is necessary for faith.

The former was directed against the medieval church, which ascribed authority to the traditions of the Church, the teachings of the Fathers, and the decisions of councils.

The latter was directed against the 'enthusiasts' of the radical Reformation, who sought direct revelation from the Spirit rather than illumination from the Word. Luther comments: 'The devil has no better way to conquer us than by leading us away from the Word and to the Spirit.... But one should hold fast to the Word and not concede the Spirit to people apart from the Word.'[281]

This warning, and the entire thrust of Reformation theology, might be dismissed as irrelevant to many of those who embrace SLSW. After all, SLSW in large part depends on direct revelation to its leaders.[282] Consequently, it could be wrongly presumed that those who allow for ongoing revelation allow also for SLSW; while those who disallow ongoing revelation will automatically dismiss SLSW.

Three brief comments are in order.[283] First, it is ironic that many of those who believe in continuing revelation are so attentive to what the Spirit is purportedly saying today and to them, and so negligent of what he has said for the last two thousand years to the wider church. Has the Spirit only recently begun speaking again after a moratorium since the first century?

Secondly, while allowing for ongoing revelation from the Spirit, Scripture is also insistent on the evaluation of all teaching which purports to come by direct revelation (e.g., 1 Cor 14:29-32; Gal 1:8; 1 Tim 4:1-6; 1 John 4:1-3). Claiming direct inspiration is inadequate; all claims must be tested and a major part of the test is conformity to Scripture.

Thirdly, there is no direct or necessary correlation between accepting ongoing revelation and embracing the teaching of SLSW. This is obvious in the roll call of prominent Pentecostal, charismatic and 'Third-Wave' Christians who would allow for the former while disallowing the latter.[284]

In the conclusion to his critique of 'health-and-wealth' theology, McConnell makes an impassioned appeal for retaining a place for ongoing revelation while recovering the Reformation doctrine of *sola Scriptura*.

> The revelatory gifts of the Spirit – prophecy, words of wisdom and knowledge – can and should have their place in the church.... [But] until we become seriously committed to the principle that all doctrine and practice must be derived from the hermeneutically sound exegesis of God's Word, our movement will remain vulnerable to an endless series of prophetic revelators and their bizarre teachings....
>
> We must reconstruct our doctrine of revelation in such a manner as to allow for the revelatory gifts of the Spirit that are our charismatic heritage, but which also clearly insists upon the Reformation principle of *sola Scriptura*.[285]

For the last twenty years or more, evangelical churches and missions have been spinning on a carousel, lurching for the brass ring which promises rapid and dramatic success in ministry. But with each revolution, the carousel spins faster and the ring moves to a new location. Can anything but a return to the principle of *sola Scriptura* deliver us from this frenzied, dizzying and unproductive ride?

There is no better summary of the Reformers' recognition of demonic powers and their confidence in the power of the Word of God than the words penned by Martin Luther over four hundred years ago:

A mighty fortress is our God,
A bulwark never failing;
Our helper He, amid the flood
Of mortal ills prevailing.
For still our ancient foe
Doth seek to work us woe;
His craft and pow'r are great,
And, armed with cruel hate,
On earth is not his equal.

Did we in our own strength confide,
Our striving would be losing;
Were not the right Man on our side,
The Man of God's own choosing.
Dost ask who that may be?

Christ Jesus, it is He;
Lord Sabaoth His name,
From age to age the same,
And He must win the battle.

And tho' this world, with devils filled,
Should threaten to undo us;
We will not fear, for God hath willed
His truth to triumph through us.
The prince of darkness grim —
We tremble not for him;
His rage we can endure,
For lo! his doom is sure,
One little word shall fell him.   (trans F. Hodge)

CHAPTER SEVEN

IN SEARCH OF A NEW PARADIGM:
SLSW & ANIMISM

Summary: While animistic faiths often affirm the existence of territorial spirits, this evidence provides little support for SLSW, for two reasons. First, even where it appears, territoriality is not a prominent feature of animism. Secondly, the cosmology of animism is incompatible with that of Christianity.

When I was conducting a seminar on the subject of territorial spirits in Singapore, one participant queried, 'Why do you have any doubts about this? We know from Chinese religion that spirits are territorial.'

This line of argument appears also in the promotional literature. In an article which has received high marks within the movement, veteran missionary Vernon Sterk surveys the beliefs of the Zinacanteco tribe of Tzotzil-speaking Indians in Chiapas, Mexico, and observes that 'all of the spirits have geographical limits for their power.'[286] On this basis he concludes, 'It is clear from empirical observation that a case can be made for the existence of territorial spirits.'[287]

The rationale is logical: Who should know more about the spirits and the demons than the people who worship them? So if animists believe that the gods are territorial, and if Christians view these gods as demonic, then it follows that demons are territorial.

In considering this evidence, we must ask two questions. First, does animism generally endorse the concept of territorial spirits? Secondly, is animism a reliable source for Christian belief and practice?

ARE ANIMISTIC SPIRITS TERRITORIAL?

There are, of course, thousands of versions of animism around the world, so it is impossible to consider even a small fraction of them all. Nor is it necessary. For while there are a great many differences between any two, on the questions addressed here they produce remarkably similar results. This is not to deny that some other version of animism might produce different results. But surely the question is not, Can we find some version of animism which suits our purposes?, but rather, Generally speaking, do animists conceive of the spirits as geographically specific?

The answer is clear and explicit: Invariably, some. That is, each form of animism (or at least the several versions which I investigated!) views some of the spirits as governing explicitly delineated and fixed geographical regions. Now the question is, What do we make of this mixed evidence?

The initial enthusiasm prompted by the discovery needs to be tempered with a sobering reality: by definition, animistic faiths believe in the existence of a great number and variety of supernatural beings. Spirits are everywhere and influence everything that happens. Within such a worldview, it is nearly inevitable that some spirits will be viewed as geographically specific. At the same time, it is notable that the majority of the spirits are not conceived to be territorial.

Chinese Folk Religion

Within Chinese animism (a mixture of Buddhism, Taoism and a preponderance of animism), there are four categories of supernatural beings: gods of heaven, gods of the underworld, gods of the earth, and ancestral spirits.

The gods of heaven include: the Jade Emperor, Gautama Buddha, the Goddess of Mercy, the Monkey God, the Sun God, the Moon Goddess, and many others (including sometimes both Jesus and the Virgin Mary). The gods of the underworld fall into three categories: judges, assistants and executioners. Ancestral spirits receive the most attention in daily rites, however: since they were once human, they are not as powerful as the deities; but they can at least be counted on to look after their descendants.

It is only the earth gods, and not all of them, which are considered to be geographically specific. Some are topographical: gods of mountains, seas and waters, or land areas. Some are ecological: gods of trees or of natural elements. Some are cultic: gods of man-made objects. And there are more besides.

Of the earth gods, only the gods of land areas are geographically specific. They are differentiated into various classes, each with jurisdiction over a different sort of realm. One type rules over Chinese settlements, another over geographical regions, others over urban or rural areas, and others over individual homes. Most important among the domestic spirits are the 'kitchen god' and the 'god of the backyard.'[288]

So does Chinese animism endorse the concept of territorial spirits? To an extent. Each backyard has a patron deity, as does each building site and each locality. Another rules over the entire city-state of Singapore. But these constitute only a small fraction of the deities. The vast bulk of the spirits in Chinese folk religion are not geographically specific. The rest are topographical, ecological, functional, celestial, chthonic or ancestral.

So if we invoke evidence from Chinese animism to establish the territoriality of demons, we face a dilemma. Can we justify citing the small portion of data which supports the theory while ignoring the bulk which undermines it?

Or must we accept the lot, and conduct spiritual warfare not only against territorial demons, but also against demons of the heavens and the underworld, of mountains, seas and waters, of trees and natural elements, of backyards and kitchens? If we begin to pick and choose, what criteria – apart from convenience – do we employ to separate the accurate from the erroneous?

Tzotzil Animism

While Tzotzil beliefs are largely different, the end result is the same. The cosmos is divided into three spheres, each with its own set of deities. The world is believed to be cubical, resting on the shoulders of the Four-Corner Gods; the sky is ruled by Father Sun and Mother Moon; the underworld is inhabited by dwarfs and monkeys.

In the domain of human life, weather patterns and land use are governed by 'the Earth Owner', a deity who lives under the ground and can be contacted in the mouth of caves. No Zinacanteco may use any of his products, such as mud, trees or lime, without conducting ceremonies to compensate him. He is essentially an agricultural god, and his worship figures prominently at crucial times in the harvest cycle.

The people are organised into social groupings of various sorts: family lineage, waterhole group, hamlet and tribe. They are watched over by ancestral spirits, whose structure matches human society. The spirits do not form a hierarchy with differentiated jurisdiction over adjoining properties, but a communal association with collective jurisdiction over the various social groupings.[289]

Sterk describes even more types of supernatural beings: functional spirits in charge of various kinds of evil, ecological spirits dwelling in rivers or streams, domestic spirits inhabiting particular houses, and cultic spirits connected with religious ceremonies and various sacred places. He notes that there is, in fact, a seemingly endless list of demons of all imaginable sorts.[290]

Are any of these deities territorial? Not in the sense required: the tribes do not divide their land into various geographical units each with its own ruling deity. The Earth Owner is associated with the ground, but he is an agricultural deity and owns all the land. The ancestral spirits serve collectively as guardians over various social groupings, but they do not inhabit the same areas as man, nor do they rule over the land on which man resides.

So in the end there is no precise equivalent for a concept of spirits which rule different areas of the tribal territory. Territorial differentiation plays such a small role in this tribe that scholarly anthropological studies fail to comment on it at all. Only those looking for this feature are likely to find it here. And to do so, it is necessary to pass over far more prominent themes in the Indian beliefs and practices.

Furthermore, there are a great number of Indian beliefs which proponents of SLSW are unlikely to endorse. On what basis do we excerpt a few details from an entire belief system and ignore the bulk of it? Can individual themes be so easily isolated, and the rest discarded? What is the criterion for distinguishing what is true among these beliefs from what is erroneous?

Myanmar Animism

Like Chinese folk religion, and in contrast to Tzotzil beliefs, Myanmar animism does view some spirits as territorial. But, as before, these are only one type of a bewildering array of supernatural beings, called 'nat'.

The only nat which could be considered strictly territorial are those which rule over various regions of the country, and each village within it. Those who travel to villages outside their native region come under the authority of the new village nat and follow local stipulations and taboos.

In addition, each person also has two hereditary nat, one passed down from the mother's side and another from the father's. These are ancestral rather than territorial: the identity of the god is fixed according to the region of family origin, not the region of residence. So migrants must continue to worship their original hereditary nat wherever they might subsequently reside.

Apart from these, there are many other sorts of supernatural beings. Deva are benevolent nat which reside in the twenty-six Buddhist heavens. Nature nat serve as custodians over forests, hills, paddy fields and other natural features. 'The Lord of the Great Mountain' is the sole house nat, guarding every home in the country. 'Public-works' nat are the spirits of people buried alive in the foundations of major buildings to watch over the structures and those who use them. There may also be personal and occupational nat.[291]

So only the village nat is truly a territorial spirit: he is worshipped by everyone currently residing in that locale, and by them alone. Yet this is only a small part of the total evidence. Can this single datum be imported into Christianity, without also bringing along ancestral nat, nature nat, house and building nat, and personal nat?

Javanese Animism

Javanese (Indonesian) popular beliefs affirm the existence of over one thousand deities and countless spirits. A standard anthropological survey divides them into four categories, only one of which includes any territorial spirits.

Chief among the 'place spirits' is Semar, the protector of the entire island of Java. *Dayang* are spirits which care for an entire social unit, such as a village. *Bahureksa* are guardians for particular locations or structures, such as buildings, forest clearings, trees, caves or wells.

Among the other sorts of supernatural beings are personal guardians and ancestral spirits which watch over their human descendants. Various types of malevolent ghosts also exist: a naked female spirit which sports a hole through her back and castrates men, a fire-spitting giant who walks about with his intestines spilling out through a hole in his belly, a male spirit that seduces women who then bear monsters, spirit children who bring illicit wealth and slow painful death, demons that enter through the soles of one's feet during sunset, and so forth.[292]

So again there is clear evidence of territorial spirits. More explicit evidence, in fact, is found in Javanese animism than in Tzotzil beliefs. But at the same time, only a minority of the spirits are territorial. And some of the attendant beliefs seem rather bizarre.

Summary

Do animists believe in territorial spirits? The answer is a qualified yes. The main qualifications are four in number. First, this applies only to some, and not to all, forms of animism. Secondly, generally only a minority of the spirits are viewed as territorial (the rest are ecological, topographical, ancestral, and so on). Thirdly, even for those which are geographically specific, this feature is rarely portrayed as their primary characteristic. (More common is an emphasis on guardianship.) This means, fourthly, that there are a host of other beliefs about the spirits and the spirit world which have nothing to do with geographical jurisdiction.[293]

Herein lies the crux of the problem. On what grounds do we highlight particular details from animism which suit our purpose, while ignoring the rest? Missionary anthropologist David Burnett comments:

> One of the basic principles of anthropology is a recognition that cultures are integrated, and that to remove one item for study in isolation can lead to a gross misunderstanding of its true meaning in context.... I

should like to stress the danger of taking random items from any culture.[294]

If we are to avoid distorting the evidence, the question to ask is not, 'Are there any details within animism which support SLSW?'; but 'How do animists perceive their gods?'

It would be a different matter if we could stand on the authority of Scripture to affirm the territoriality of spirits. In that case we could use animistic beliefs merely for illustration. But appealing to animism to establish the existence of territorial spirits raises two problems. For one, territoriality plays a subordinate role in animism. For the other, animism may not be a reliable foundation for Christian theology. The latter issue repays further exploration.

ANIMISM AND CHRISTIANITY: COMPATIBLE PARADIGMS?

Is animism a credible source for Christian theology? Are the two systems even compatible, either in whole or in part?

The Excluded Middle

More than a decade ago, missiologist Paul Hiebert appealed to animism to illustrate a shift in his own thinking. His Western training had equipped him intellectually to present rational arguments for faith in Christ. But the most urgent needs of the Indians to whom he ministered were not philosophical. Instead, they clamoured for help in defending themselves against illnesses and misfortune brought on by angry spirits.

Through this experience, Hiebert came to recognise that Western Christianity had developed a worldview comprising two tiers, with supernatural forces restricted to heaven, humans confined on earth, and little direct contact between the two. Indian thinking, he discovered, had a large middle realm, where supernatural forces acted on the natural domain, either for good or for ill.

'For me,' Hiebert concludes, 'the middle zone did not really exist. Unlike Indian villagers, I had given little thought to spirits of this world, to local ancestors and ghosts, or to the souls of animals.'[295] This discrepancy prompted him to call for 'a theology of God in human history', including 'a theology of divine guidance, provision and healing; of ancestors, spirits and invisible powers of this world; and of suffering, misfortune and death.'[296]

So animism can alert Christians to errors in their worldviews. But do we then adopt aspects of animism to fill the omissions in our theology?

Hiebert did not. Indeed, he warned originally, and has repeated more recently, that the pendulum may swing to the opposite extreme: from rationalistic Christianity to animistic Christianity.[297]

The Overextended Middle

While there is a fundamental and crucial difference between rationalism and biblical Christianity, there is no less difference between animism and biblical Christianity. With respect to the present topic, they differ over the functions of God, of spirits and of man.

Many animistic faiths affirm the role of a Creator God, or at least of a Lord over the universe. Almost invariably, however, this powerful deity has withdrawn from the world. Christianity will have none of this: God the Creator constantly upholds the world; Christ the Incarnate has lived among us and now intercedes for us; the Spirit is present in the church and indwells the people of God.

With absent or preoccupied deities, animism turns over most of life to the spirits. All misfortune has a supernatural cause: every illness, every madness, every poor crop or economic setback is caused by an offended spirit or by a human curse. There is no concept of a sovereign God who controls all events, or of a fallen natural order in which evil and illness occur without direct intervention by malicious spirits.

Given the absence of an actively involved Sovereign Deity, and faced with the constant threat of evil spirits, human efforts play a crucial role in animism. Diviners determine the identity of the spirit causing the misfortune; shaman devise techniques for thwarting the demons. The naming of evil spiritual forces, the appeal to benevolent powers, the design of rituals, and the observance of taboos are all essential aspects of animistic techniques to guarantee human safety in an unpredictable world.[298]

These three characteristics of animism are interrelated, as Hiebert points out:

> [In animism] most things that happen are brought about ... by spirits, ancestors, ghosts, magic, witchcraft and the stars. It is a world in which God is distant and in which humans are at the mercy of good and evil powers and must defend themselves by means of prayers and chants, charms, medicines and incantations. Power, not truth, is the central human concern in this worldview.[299]

These characteristics also highlight the increasing danger which encroaching animism pose for historic Christianity.

When the key to ministry success depends on a particular type, pattern or formula of prayer, then animism is not far behind. When effectiveness depends on identifying and using spirit names, magic is at work. When power is opposed to truth, and then is found in technique, the transformation is complete.

Thus, the recent trumpeting of a need for a paradigm shift in evangelical Christianity entails a false dichotomy. The choice is not, as assumed, between rationalistic Christianity and biblical Christianity. There are at least three choices: rationalistic Christianity, biblical Christianity, and spiritistic Christianity. Due to this false dichotomy, the warnings about rationalism, which would have been very valuable twenty years ago, now threaten to encourage and justify the current swing to spiritism.

CONCLUSION

So there are two problems with invoking animism in support of demon territoriality. For one, territoriality plays a subordinate role in animism. For the other, animism is not a reliable foundation for Christian theology.

In closing, four ironies might be noted in the current appeal to animism as a basis for, or in confirmation of, spirit territoriality.

First, within animism, spirits are often viewed as neutral; that is, they assist people who respect them, and harm those who offend them. Christianity, however, views them as consistently demonic. Thus, animists worship the spirits; Christians wage war against them. If we reject the testimony of animism on such a central point, how can we endorse its beliefs in more peripheral matters, such as the boundaries of jurisdiction?

Secondly, both Christianity and animism recognise the possibility of demon possession and the practice of magic or shamanism.[300] Notably, where the two religions agree, at least in part, we do not appeal to animism in support of Christian teaching. But where the silence of Scripture leaves us with no reliable criterion by which to distinguish truth from error, animism is used to fill in the gaps.

Thirdly, it has widely been noted that the belief in territoriality is common among isolated rural peoples. Yet as such cultures break up through modernisation, and people migrate to the cities in search of employment, the link between spirits and land becomes weaker and is finally abandoned.[301] But in this instance, missiologists from industrial-ised, urbanised countries appeal to rural, agricultural societies for theo-logical guidance, at the same time as those societies are moving away from agrarian beliefs.

Finally, perhaps the greatest irony is the promotion of belief in territorial demons by Western academics. The 'high' forms of the major world religions (such as Islam, Judaism, Christianity and Buddhism) give little place or power to spirits. But each exists also in folk versions, where it is combined with, and distorted by, animism.

Academics, professional theologians and ordained clergy of all religions consistently make Herculean efforts to purify beliefs and practices by excising animistic accretions from populist faith.[302] But within evangelical Christianity a few prominent missiologists are in danger of moving in the opposite direction.

In short, the attempt to support SLSW from animism is both futile and hazardous. It is futile because the desired evidence comes from animism only through the tendentious use of sources. It is hazardous because animism and Christianity comprise two widely divergent worldviews.

There is ground for concern that SLSW has assimilated elements of an animistic worldview.[303] There is ground for even greater concern that the appeal to animism recognises these affinities, and actually endorses – rather than expunges – them. When a teaching finds more support from animism than from Scripture, Christopaganism looms near.

Nevertheless, these trends may largely reflect an overreaction to the rationalistic tendencies of recent decades. If so, they will presumably moderate with time. While grounds for considerable concern remain, we must not forget that proponents of SLSW have performed an important service in alerting evangelicalism to its recently insipid and careless attitude toward prayer and toward demons, as well as its lethargy in the practice of spiritual warfare.

At the same time, we must be alert to the danger of overreaction, the common phenomenon of swinging from one extreme to another. We must seek the safe waters of biblical Christianity between the shoals of rationalism and the cliffs of spiritism.

CHAPTER EIGHT

DOES IT WORK?
SLSW & THE EMPIRICAL EVIDENCE

Summary: Arguments from experience are admissible, but more careful selection and sober evaluation of the data are necessary before the case study evidence can be persuasive. Upon closer examination, even enthusiastic proponents apparently do not intend to portray SLSW as a sufficient – or even as an especially effective – cause of church growth in Latin America.

In the end, the strongest justification for SLSW is that it works.[304] More than this, its effectiveness is unprecedented: '*God is now giving His missionary force the greatest power boost it has had since the time that William Carey went to India in 1793*'![305]

Thus, warfare prayer is credited with bringing down the Berlin Wall and the Iron Curtain, with penetrating Albania with the gospel, with deposing dictators like Manuel Noriega of Nicaragua, with lowering the crime rate of American cities, and with reviving the economies of Third-World nations.[306]

Other reports are more detailed, though no less exciting. Within three years, one church grows from 500 to 2,500 members, and another from 200 to 1,600 members. A stagnant church of 30 members leaps to 3,000 through the use of warfare prayer. Another church grows at a moderate pace by employing church growth principles, but jumps quickly to one thousand members with the use of warfare prayer. 'How did mediocre evangelism become effective evangelism? The answer was the frontline application of strategic-level spiritual warfare.'[307]

Argentine businessman and evangelist Carlos Annacondia is commended as perhaps 'the most effective crusade evangelist of all time.'[308] What is he doing that other evangelists are not? Warfare prayer!

In the absence of biblical evidence or historical precedent, and in view of the emphasis proponents place on proven effectiveness, the case studies play a crucial role. So this evidence deserves careful consideration.

The reports cannot simply be accepted at face value, without confirmation, substantiation or evaluation. Who has not experienced the confusion that can result when a message is passed through intermediaries? Yet some of these reports are third- or even fourth-hand by the time they reach print. Did the event occur as reported, or has the account been distorted in the process of transmission?

If the event has been reported accurately, has it also been interpreted properly? There is a certain naive realism which assumes that the meaning of events is transparently clear. Yet all events require interpretation, all the more so when trying to unravel their cause(s). Some of these accounts give evidence of common errors in interpretation.

Finally, many of the stories originate from South America, where Protestantism has been growing rapidly over the last fifty years. Consequently, there is a wealth of literature, from populist Church Growth analyses to scholarly sociological reflections, on the factors which contribute to growth. This provides a helpful background for interpreting recent events and claims.

The call to evaluate empirical data does not reflect unbridled scepticism; it is merely responsible stewardship. After all, for the last three decades great numbers of churches pinned their hopes on the Church Growth movement, a strategy which equally suffered from a lack of biblical or historical evidence, but which also claimed preponderant empirical support. Now, after the investment of enormous amounts of time, energy and funds, even former promoters tell us that the methods have not worked.[309] Such frankness is commendable; but mistakes do not breed confidence, especially when a similar rationale is employed to justify several different strategies over two decades!

So it is important to ask: Did the events happen as recounted? Did they happen for the reasons given? Or were other, more likely and more significant, factors at work?

ARE THE REPORTS RELIABLE?

God is doing much at present, and some suggest that he is doing it through SLSW. But not all the evidence cited is of the same value. Some is irrelevant; some is inherently dubious; some, beyond confirmation; some simply erroneous. But once the debris is removed, some solid evidence remains and it bears further consideration.

Among the irrelevant data are occasions when evangelism has been especially effective after a time of prolonged prayer. Since its inception the church has prayed in conjunction with evangelism. There should be nothing unusual about this practice, or surprising about its effectiveness. In the present discussion, however, such evidence is irrelevant, for it establishes merely that God answers prayer, a point which is hardly in dispute. To support SLSW, case studies must first correspond to its distinctive practices.

Much of the empirical evidence is unconvincing simply because it is haphazardly collected or cited. If, for instance, social violence can be overcome through SLSW, then presumably this should be apparent in the genocides of Rwanda, Bosnia, and Cambodia, more than in the crime rate of Los Angeles during the Olympics. If SLSW is more effective than traditional spiritual warfare in stimulating stagnant economies, this would be more evident in Bangladesh or Laos than in Argentina. If warfare prayer is more effective than intercessory prayer in relieving political oppression, then this should be demonstrated in North Korea and China, not just in Eastern Europe.

In the category of inherently dubious evidence, pride of place belongs to the account of tourists praying against KGB headquarters in Moscow. Four years after this prayer, we are told, the Soviet Union collapsed and the KGB fell from power.[310] Only a convinced optimist could accord that particular time of prayer a special role in the events which transpired four years later. Surely the credit belongs to the prayers of God's suffering people uttered over the previous seventy years, even if it was not warfare prayer (see Rev 6:10; 8:4; 12:11).

A classic and often repeated example of evidence that is beyond confirmation is the story of a missionary serving in a town straddling the border between Uruguay and Brazil. The main street in the town runs straight down the border. The missionary noted that people presented with tracts on the Uruguay side would refuse them. Once the same people crossed over to the Brazil side, they would receive the tracts with profuse thanks. The missionary prayed over this puzzle and God purportedly revealed that the ruling spirits had been broken on one side, but not on the other.[311]

Some of the details in this story cry out for further investigation. Was someone actually so careless as to bind the spirits over one half the town, and leave the other half intact? Do the geographical limitations of territorial spirits correspond precisely to the recent, shifting and often ill-defined political boundaries of nations, extending even to one side of a street? How is it that the spirits are stronger in secular Uruguay than in spiritistic Brazil?

But the point is not simply that this story is inherently implausible; merely that such questions cannot be answered because the source of the story is so remote, both in geography and in transmission. It is no simple matter to confirm a report which derives from an unnamed missionary in an unspecified town thousands of miles away, conveyed via an international mission leader who in turn is cited by another missiologist.[312]

Such caution may be dismissed as sub-Christian cynicism, but in the one case which I am able to verify, wariness is certainly in order. The story is told of stagnating churches in the town of Mallakka, Malaysia. A prophet purportedly came from England and identified the cause of the lethargy. It turns out that Jesuit missionary Francis Xavier was poorly received by the townspeople more than four hundred years earlier, so he went up a nearby mountain, and shook the dust from his sandals as a curse against the town. The English prophet took a group of people up the mountain and broke the curse. As a result, the churches began growing again.[313]

For most readers of this story, the incident would be beyond confirmation. Yet 'Mallakka' is my wife's hometown, and we have spent the last decade within driving distance. Plenty of documentary evidence is available locally on Xavier's ministry, but its only effect is to underline a series of errors in the account.

First, the spelling is wrong: Melaka is the current Malay spelling; Malacca, the colonial British; Malakka, Malaka, and Mallacca were all known in previous centuries;[314] but I have found no record of Mallakka.

The topography is also inaccurate. There is no mountain within a hundred miles of the town, though there is a small hill near the city centre. (The city survey department reports that St. Paul's Hill is little over 100 feet high.)

The history is erroneous. The church existed in Melaka before Xavier arrived, and has been growing in the four hundred years since his departure. In fact, all the standard Protestant denominations (Presbyterian, Anglican, Methodist, Brethren, Baptist, Assembly of God) have entered during this time.[315]

It is not even certain when or why Xavier brushed the dust off his feet as a rebuke. There is a reliable report that he did so while departing after his first visit in 1545-46; then the cause was the persistent refusal of Portuguese settlers to marry their native concubines.[316] A second, widespread, though not entirely trustworthy, report places the event at the end of his final visit in 1552, when it was directed specifically against the Captain of the Port who subverted his attempts to visit China.[317]

Finally, the interpretation of the act is completely wrong. This action is a divinely approved rebuke, warning of coming judgement on the unrepentant, not a curse which prevents people from repenting (see Mark 6:11; Luke 9:5). Xavier appealed specifically to the relevant Gospel texts in his farewell sermon. Despite exhaustive research, leading Xavier scholar Georg Schurhammer uncovered no evidence to support the report of a curse on the city, which he dismisses as a 'later legend'.[318]

In any event, while some churches in Melaka are growing moderately (and some are not, as in many places around the world), there is no evidence of either dramatic revival or spectacular numbers of conversions in recent years. Indeed, it is Islam, rather than Christianity, which predominates both numerically and politically.

So on all points this report is unreliable: from the spelling, to the topography, the history, the event, the interpretation and the results. I have not deliberately selected the least credible report in the hopes of discounting all. This is simply the only account that I am able to verify. The inaccuracy of this report does not inspire confidence where independent avenues of confirmation are unavailable.

It would nonetheless be illegitimate to discount all reports of growth following SLSW. That is not my intent. I seek merely to establish that credulity is ill-advised.[319] There is an important qualitative difference between anecdotes and case studies, and a further distinction between case studies and social-scientific analysis. In the case of SLSW, much of the empirical data is anecdotal. While scepticism should be avoided, some measure of discretion is in order.[320]

Which raises the question of why there are so few stories that can be verified. Most readers cannot be expected to confirm events reported from Asia or Latin America. But they could check those occurring in their vicinity. This is no trifling matter for a teaching which promises a technique for powerful ministry and which depends so heavily upon empirical data for validation. Wagner acknowledged the problem in the early days:

> Research of territorial spirits is so new that the case studies that have surfaced tend to get told over and over again. I have no doubt that as time goes by credible stories of breaking powers over areas, both small and large, will multiply.[321]

In the past seven years empirical trials have been conducted around the world; the new reports should have been forthcoming. Indeed, if this method of prayer is all that it claims to be, we shall presumably not need second-hand reports from distant lands. Given the large numbers now practising warfare prayer, the results should be evident all around.

Returning to the initial question, Are the reports reliable?, the answer is often disappointing. Some reports have nothing specifically to do with SLSW. Others are inherently dubious. Most cannot be confirmed. Some which can be confirmed turn out to be false. Nevertheless, there is at least one large region in the world where the number of practising Christians has grown dramatically, and where the growth has been frequently attributed to SLSW: Latin America, and especially Argentina. But while the facts are certain, the interpretation is not.

IS THE INTERPRETATION OF EXPERIENCE CREDIBLE?
There can be no doubt that the growth of Protestantism in Latin America over the last century has been phenomenal. Once the facts are agreed, attention shifts to interpretation: Why is the church growing? Is this growth due in particular to SLSW, at least to some significant extent? The questions of fact and interpretation are different and must be kept distinct. Unfortunately, once the former is resolved, the latter is commonly assumed.

The citation of this evidence usually involves one of three common fallacies. The first is question-begging. This occurs when advocates point to evidence of rapid growth, and immediately attribute this to SLSW, without even demonstrating that SLSW was widely or commonly practised before the growth occurred. This first error assumes both subsequence and consequence.

The second fallacy is to confuse subsequence with consequence. Once it is demonstrated that SLSW was practised before the growth occurred, it cannot simply be assumed that the growth was due to SLSW. There are many factors affecting conversion, and it is not always easy to determine the most important one, or even to unravel the various contributory factors.

The third fallacy is the tendentious selection and interpretation of data. The meaning of events is not self-evident. Explanations involve interpretation and correlation of data. Often prior assumptions impinge on this process, whether consciously or unconsciously. Data can be shaped to fit preconceived theories, so that a particular conclusion is predetermined. So it is important to seek alternative explanations, not to settle quickly on any one.

This section reviews the Latin American experience, seeking evidence: first, that SLSW was conducted before times of spectacular growth; secondly, that the growth that followed can be reliably traced to the practice of SLSW; and, thirdly, that this interpretation provides the best explanation of the data.

Was SLSW Practised Before the Growth Occurred?

Most of the SLSW case studies from Latin America come from Argentina.[322] Yet, ironically, Argentina was neither the first country in the continent to experience rapid growth, nor is it the country where growth has been the fastest or the broadest. Obviously if SLSW is the cause for the growth, this should be demonstrated in the areas of early and vigorous growth.

Thus, for example, any explanation for Protestant growth in Argentina must also be able to account for the earlier, faster, and greater growth in Brazil, Chile, Guatemala, Nicaragua, Haiti, Jamaica, and Puerto Rico.

In Brazil the steep acceleration in growth began in the 1930s, so that by 1942 it was probably the fastest growing wing of the world-wide church.[323] By 1987, during the infancy of SLSW, Brazil was already 20% Protestant, double the 1980 figure. At that time, Protestants accounted for 30% of the population in Guatemala, 20% in Nicaragua, and 15-20% in Chile. By 1989, the Assemblies of God in Brazil had twenty times as many members as their sister body in Argentina. In Mexico there were twice as many as Pentecostals as in Argentina.[324]

Yet I could find no sources that date SLSW to the beginning of this explosive growth or to the rapid expansion of the Protestant Church in these other countries. At the risk of tautology, if SLSW – or any other particular technique – is especially effective in promoting church growth, this would need to be demonstrated from the countries where the church growth has been especially effective.

Even within Argentina, there have been three notable periods of growth over the last century. Protestant penetration began in the late nineteenth century. The first indigenous breakthrough occurred under the Plymouth Brethren in the 1920s. A dramatic upswing followed the evangelistic rallies by the Assemblies of God evangelist Tommy Hicks in 1954. In the last decade since the end of the Falklands War, the trend toward explosive growth noted elsewhere in Latin America has finally come to Argentina.

Was SLSW practised in conjunction with the earlier growth spurts? Apparently not; at least I have found no author to suggest that it was. So how is this growth to be explained? Could the same explanation account for the more recent growth?

Was SLSW the Cause for Subsequent Growth?
The confusion of subsequence and consequence is apparent in some of the anecdotes recounted at the beginning of this chapter. Carlos Annacondia is perhaps 'the most effective crusade evangelist of all time,' purportedly due to his practice of warfare prayer.[325] (If so, then presumably now that others have adopted his methods, he shall have more rivals!)

Yet only two pages earlier, it was acknowledged that Argentina is 'ripe for the gospel message' because of a number of national catastrophes: the loss of the Falklands War, oppressive military rule, economic stagnation and runaway inflation.[326] Given that Annacondia began his first public crusade in the midst of these catastrophes, and given that ministry styles and methods are multi-faceted, can his success confidently be attributed to one ministry practice above all others, and to ministry technique more than to social context?

Employing church growth principles, Edgardo Silvoso had become a spectacularly effective crusade evangelist before he had ever heard of SLSW. Then he began a three-year evangelistic outreach into the city of Resistencia, combining extensive training and prayer, church growth techniques, and strategic-level spiritual warfare. Hundreds of healings and exorcisms were reported, eighteen churches were started, and the number of evangelicals in the city doubled.[327] From this report, is it possible to conclude that SLSW is more effective than traditional spiritual warfare, or that the response is due more to a one-day seminar on warfare prayer, than to the preceding one year spent in prayer and training?

These incidents feature prominently in the argument for SLSW. But in each case, many factors affect the growth of the church. Consequently, it is inadequate to demonstrate that SLSW was practised before the growth. Rather, it is necessary to demonstrate further that the growth is due in some particular sense to the practice of SLSW, more than to one (or more) of the myriad other factors.

What Other Explanations Exist?
The distorting effect of prior assumptions on the interpretation of data is conspicuous in attempts to explain the growth of Protestantism in Latin America. Peter Wagner, for example, has offered three different interpretations of this phenomenon over the last twenty-five years, each of which corresponded to his theological presuppositions at the time.

As early as 1973, and then again in 1986, Wagner identified *nine* 'major factors causing church growth among Latin American Pentecostals.'[328] If nothing else, this long list calls into question the tendency to attribute growth to any single factor or method, SLSW included.

But there is something else. In 1973, during his conservative evangelical stage, Wagner stressed the work of the Holy Spirit in regeneration, and played down the role of miracles.[329] By 1986, however, during his 'power evangelism' stage, he concluded that the work of the Holy Spirit through signs and wonders is 'the first and most essential dynamic underlying Pentecostal growth.'[330]

In 1986, warfare prayer received only a brief mention, alongside healing and other similar phenomena. But by 1992, Wagner identified this practice as the key to the growth of Protestantism in Latin America.[331]

Whichever view may be correct, the changing analyses illustrate the importance of prior assumptions in the evaluation of evidence, and the decisive role of premises in interpretation. The data never changed: over the entire period, Pentecostal and charismatic churches were the fastest growing. What changed was the experience of the interpreter. When examining the empirical data it is crucial to note that 'bare facts' do not exist. Data requires selection, not to mention interpretation, and both introduce the possibility of significant subjectivity.

A SOCIAL-SCIENCE PERSPECTIVE

Proponents of SLSW claim that the social sciences see 'culture *as it appears to be*, while spiritual mapping attempts to see culture *as it really is.*'[332] Given the failure of SLSW to provide credible explanations, those interested in understanding the reasons for the growth of Protestantism would do well to reconsider social science analyses.[333]

Admittedly reductionistic in omitting consideration of God as a cause of growth, sociological and anthropological investigations otherwise follow a more careful methodology and reach more convincing conclusions than populist evangelical missions literature.[334] While there is not space here to do justice to this material, a brief survey may at least glance at the sorts of factors which the social sciences have identified as conducive to growth.

The Influence of Social Context

As might be expected, the basic assumption of the social sciences is that social context plays a significant role in human decision-making, including choice of religion and conversion.[335] But this is not merely an assumption: it is borne out by the evidence.

Thus, in his analysis of the massive revival in Indonesia from 1965–1968, Willis surveys the church growth methods which facilitated growth, but this takes up only one-fifth of the book. The rest discusses structural and contextual factors which created an environment conducive to growth.

This emphasis is intentional. Comparing the methods employed by each denomination with the rate of growth enjoyed by each, he notes that, 'All the denominations grew, regardless of methodology used or concept of evangelism followed.' At the same time, some grew considerably faster than others. His conclusion: 'Religio-cultural, political, and sociological factors played a larger role in church growth than methods; but methodological factors played a significant role in slowing or speeding the rate of growth.'[336]

That is to say, church growth methods, such as those identified above for Latin America, can facilitate or impede growth, but they explain neither the possibility of conversion, nor the preference for one religion over another, much less the collective attraction toward a novel religion. Willis adds:

> The fantastic growth of churches ministering to the Javanese, and the eleven reasons cited for that growth support our basic thesis that God prepares people and countries for response to the gospel through a confluence of anthropological, political, sociological, economic, cultural, and religious factors.[337]

When the appropriate social factors converged, the church in Indonesia grew precipitously for some three years; when the factors then diverged, the growth tapered off.[338]

Sowing seed is essential, and some methods are better than others; but all is of no avail if the ground is not plowed and ready for planting. Methods are not to be rejected as useless; but the best methods in the world are of little use if the context is unfavourable to change.

The Social Context and Church Growth in Argentina

Ironically, given his flamboyant expectations for SLSW, even Wagner acknowledges the importance of social context in the recent growth of Protestantism in Argentina:

> Of all the nations in Latin America, Argentina, along with a few others such as Uruguay and Venezuela, had not seen the rapid growth of Protestant or evangelical churches so characteristic of the continent as a whole....
>
> A dramatic change came with the Falkland Islands war against Great Britain in 1982.... The British victory caused a radical change in Argentine social psychology.... Their national pride was shattered.... They were ready to try something new![339]

Actually, he goes on to suggest, the social context had begun to change many years earlier, through economic mismanagement and oppressive military rule. 'Little wonder,' he concludes, 'the nation is now ripe for the gospel message.'[340]

Wagner never explains how these comments about the crucial role of social context are to be integrated with his statements about the crucial role of warfare prayer, let alone with his earlier two analyses of church-growth methods in Latin America. But at least this version of the events finds ample support in the sociological literature.

The Social Context of Protestant Growth in Latin America

Much has been written of late concerning the spread of evangelicalism in Latin America, and there is neither the space nor the need to survey it here. But a brief introduction to one of the best recent works may at least give some feel for the insights which sociology offers for understanding the process of religious conversion. In *Tongues of Fire: The Explosion of Protestantism in Latin America*, sociologist David Martin draws attention to the socio-cultural-economic factors which make the growth of Protestantism (and especially Pentecostalism) possible, attractive and prevalent.

How Is Conversion Possible?

The growth of Protestantism within any traditionally non-Protestant context presupposes a breakdown of the union of nation and religion, people and faith, community and congregation. This fragmentation can result from a variety of factors (such as immigration, loss of traditional leadership, or national calamity), but undoubtedly the most common modern causes – and the most relevant in the Latin American context – are industrialisation and urbanisation.

In short, '*as the sacred canopy in Latin America is rent and the all-encompassing system cracks, evangelical Christianity pours in and by its own autonomous native power creates free social space.*'[341] Like a seed which takes root in the crack of a concrete walkway, Protestantism could enter Latin America only where the monolith of culture had already fractured. Like the seed, once it enters, it expands until the crack becomes a crevice.

Conversions come mostly among those who have left the constraints of traditional society. Some have achieved independence through small business ventures or through the purchase of land. Others have inherited independence through marginalisation, resulting, for instance, from their rural location or ethnic identity (such as immigrants or native Indians). Probably the largest portion have independence thrust upon them, as agro-business forces them from small family farms into urban ghettos.[342] Such people have nothing to lose by the adoption of a new religion, either because they have nothing to begin with, or because they have already achieved a measure of economic independence. Instead, they have much to gain.

Why Is Conversion Attractive?

Religious motivation is complex, but for the most part, people respond to a message which meets their needs, communicated in language they can understand, and reflecting values that agree with their own. This has long been realised, and is being replayed in Latin America.

The new religion provides advance on all fronts. Culturally, it offers links with American Protestantism, at a time when the United States has been a leading power militarily, economically, and technologically. Socially, democratic relationships prevail within the local church, with various classes mingling equally. Religiously, it ensures safety from the spirit world at a considerably lower cost and through more convenient means than traditional spiritism. Economically, the new religion imparts values of hard work and frugality, thus supporting a culture of social mobility.

Protestantism provides education, emotional release, the status of U.S. goods, new networks to replace those lost in urbanisation, a reduction of family violence, populist enthusiasm, a gentler spiritism, indirect and non-violent social change. Martin summarises:

[Pentecostalism] offers participation, mutual support, emotional release, a sense of identity and dignity, and though authoritarian it does not offer authority to those who also have status in the outside world. Pentecostalism provides a substitute society, and within that society cares largely for its own, by way of schools, orphanages, homes for the elderly and informal employment exchanges.[343]

In short, Latin American Pentecostalism is religion for the disenfranchised but ambitious lower-class.

Why Does Conversion Spread?

In the previous century, elite Protestant denominations sought entry to Latin America through social and economic development. Entire networks were established, comprising churches, schools, seminaries, hospitals, orphanages, publishing houses and retreat centres. This created significant good-will throughout society, and won converts among the middle classes. But there were strict limits to the potential of this methodology. The resources were never sufficient to reach the illiterate masses, and the orientation was too intellectual to appeal.

Pentecostalism offers the same benefits as traditional Protestantism in a form which is accessible to the masses:

Pentecostalism ... enables many of its followers to achieve a power in their lives which can simultaneously infuse them with the possibility of 'betterment' and of new goods of every kind, spiritual and material, and also put them in touch with spiritual charges and discharges lodged deep in the indigenous culture, black, Indian or Hispanic.[344]

In cultures with long spiritual roots, 'Pentecostalism offers the old fiesta in the form of lively worship, the old trances in the form of spiritual ecstasy, and the old networks in the form of the brotherhood.'[345]

Pentecostalism also manages to avoid the alienating effects of higher education. Among cultures which are informal, spontaneous, and oral, it forsakes linear, intellectual preaching for gripping stories of the works of God. Ministry style is not populist by accident or by conscious intention, but by birth. Leadership is now indigenous, and the fastest growing churches are often independent and recently founded.[346]

Rising through the ranks, rather than trained in graduate schools of theology, these pastors instinctively sense what fits their context, largely because it also fits them. Indigenous, working-class leadership is crucial to rapid growth, partly because it ensures culturally appropriate ministry, and partly because it provides yet another avenue of upward mobility, and another model of success for the masses to emulate.

CONCLUSION

This summary does no justice to the complexity of social change, the sophistication of social science research, or the breadth and depth of Martin's analysis of Latin America. Nonetheless, it should suffice to highlight the contrast between the anecdotes of SLSW and the extensive argumentation and careful interpretation of social science.

Though phrased in the aura of social-scientific terminology (such as 'hypothesis', 'evidence', and 'research'), SLSW does not employ a rigorous method. The failure to critique and confirm case studies before publication leads to the inclusion of clearly unreliable reports, and therefore to uncertainty about the reliability of any report. Moreover, the assignment of particular interpretations to these reports is often arbitrary.

Admittedly, the social sciences are unlikely to explain every aspect of the growth of Protestantism in Latin America, but they explain a whole lot more than SLSW does.

CHAPTER NINE

IF NOT SLSW, WHAT THEN?
A BIBLICAL AND EFFECTIVE ALTERNATIVE

*Summary: While the theory and practice of SLSW are indefensible,
the proposal at least highlights recent laxity in the evangelical
practice of spiritual warfare. The solution is not to be found in
formulating a new teaching or technique, but in returning to long-
standing, but recently overlooked, theology and practice.*

So far this critique has reached consistently negative conclusions. From all angles – biblical, theological, historical, sociological, or empirical – there is little to commend either the theory of territorial spirits or the practice of warfare prayer. The evidence adduced in support of SLSW is sometimes irrelevant, generally tendentious, largely misinterpreted, and consistently invalid. This is a strong verdict and affords no pleasure, but it is demanded by the importance of the issue and the clarity of the data.

The sheer amount and scope of data invoked in favour of SLSW has required such an extensive response that other, unintended conclusions could be read into this critique. Most worrisome among them would be the supposition that Satan is no threat to the evangelist and missionary. The rejection of one particular method in no way implies that spiritual warfare as a whole lacks urgency.

For all its faults, SLSW does at least call attention to the recent laxity in the evangelical practice of spiritual warfare and intercessory prayer. It is true, to our shame, that over the last several decades in particular, evangelical evangelism, discipleship, and missions strategy has often been seduced by the promise that the key to spiritual success lies in improved technique.

The traditional priority assigned to preaching, prayer and spiritual warfare was usurped in the 1960s and 1970s by means and methods, such as church growth principles, management techniques, and marketing strategies. The over-emphasis on otherwise useful insights and tools often led to a relative neglect of the divinely ordained means for conveying spiritual truth and power.

The church has long been engaged in cross-cultural mission and has practised spiritual warfare for much of that time. Rather than inventing new methods, it is more sensible – if less exciting – to return to the tested and proven.

This chapter draws attention to one example of traditional spiritual warfare: the ministry of James Fraser to the Lisu of south-west China (1909–1938), under the auspices of the China Inland Mission (now OMF International).

THE TACTICS OF THE EVIL ONE

When James Fraser arrived in the far-western region of Yunnan province in 1909, evangelism had already led to mass conversions among the despised mountain peoples in the eastern region of the province.

His interest was in the western district and the Lisu there.

> I was very much led out in prayer for these people, right from the begin-
> ning. Something seemed to draw me to them; and the desire in my heart
> grew until it became a burden that God would give us hundreds of con-
> verts among the Lisu of our western district.[347]

At the age of twenty-three, Fraser made his first trip into the mountains which were to be his home for the rest of his life.

In describing the initial years of his ministry, and the winning of the
first few converts, his daughter and biographer Eileen Crossman notes:

> The prince of this world does not easily cede his territory to the people of
> God. The mountains had been the stronghold of Satan for countless
> centuries: they were not to be lightly invaded. Persuasion to pay half-
> hearted lip-service to God for a while would be a relatively harmless exer-
> cise.... But if the Spirit of the Living God were to regenerate the hearts of
> these people and set up His Kingdom there, it would be another matter....
> The enemy would make an onslaught against any such possibility. He
> would attack the messenger, his message and all who gave ear to it.[348]

Over the next twenty-five years of ministry, Fraser would gain considerable experience and insight into Satan's power and tactics, whether
against the converts, the message, or himself.

Attacks On New Converts

In a vast province with so few workers, itinerant ministry was unavoid-
able, especially in the early years. But it presented critical obstacles to
the work. With no more than a week at a time to spend in most villages
or hamlets, Fraser found that new converts faced severe testing after
his departure.

The Lisu were particularly bound to demon worship through fear
of physical illness. After one family converted, the youngest son fell
ill. They prayed for his recovery but he became worse. In desperation, they sought help from a spirit medium. At his advice, they offered
an animal to appease the offended spirit, and the boy recovered, tem-
porarily.

As a consequence, however, he and the youngest brother were
possessed by demons and demanded obeisance: 'I will show you earth
people whether I have power or not!' Shortly thereafter the youngest
died. Later an elder brother quarrelled with his wife, and she committed

suicide; then that son ran away from the family home.[349]

For Fraser, this was something of an awakening. Never before had he come up against such vigorous demonic opposition.

> After a lifetime of service to the Evil One, these people tried, in a blundering way, to break free and worship God, through Jesus Christ. Then came the trial of their faith. Satan raged. He got his knife into those who dared to question his authority in his Lisu kingdom. He was successful.... His rebels gave him back their allegiance. First, then, for the candy, to show what a kind master he is – the boy got better; then with sevenfold fury for the whip![350]

Renunciation in the face of serious illness proved to be a frequent problem.

Demonstrations of Occult Power

In another Lisu region, Fraser saw a dramatic manifestation of demonic power. To appease a local spirit, the local shaman had devised a ritual in which a dozen or more swords would be sharpened and fixed to poles like the rungs on a ladder. Several men would prepare through fasting and purifying baths over the course of three days. Then, under great excitation, they would ascend the ladder with bare feet. Fraser commented:

> They all tell me that no man so 'prepared' is ever injured, though they frequently suffer from fear beforehand. They say too that no one 'unprepared' would dare attempt it, for the blades would just about cut his feet in pieces. When at the top on a kind of platform, they look down with glaring eyes and in unearthly tones give messages from the spirit. At times they make a huge fire also, in which they burn iron chains until red hot – then in some kind of paroxysm they pick them up and throw them round their shoulders. In this case also they say that no harm comes to them.[351]

Particularly noteworthy is the Lisu perspective on these displays of power. Fraser continues:

> You might suppose that onlookers regard the whole thing as a kind of entertainment but this is far from the case. They all say that they wish they knew how to get rid of the burden; but they *must* do it, whether they want to or not.[352]

Several in these villages professed faith in Christ, but Fraser was left with a deepened sense of the malicious power of the evil one, and a renewed urgency for preaching the deliverance which comes through Christ.

Opposition to the Message

In the district of Tantsah, Fraser found the people highly responsive. Anticipating the day when many would turn to Christ, he recognised the need for books, and thus the need to devise a written script. This would take consultation with other missionary colleagues involved in similar tribal work across the border in Burma.

Before leaving on this journey of several weeks, he called together the leading Lisu to ascertain their willingness to follow Christ. On the condition that he would return to be their teacher, the majority expressed the intention to become Christians.

In his brief absence, though, he received disturbing reports. On his trip back, messengers actually met him outside the town, begging him not to return. Though he had been away only one month, the situation had entirely reversed. The dominant Chinese majority of the town had circulated wild rumours about his hidden motives, accusing him of being an agent of the British government. They pressured the Lisu into signing an agreement that they would neither turn Christian nor permit him to reside among them; otherwise, their properties would be confiscated.

While the Lisu apparently wanted him to return, they did not dare to face this opposition. As he mulled over the situation, Fraser saw behind the ethnic hostility and perceived the interfering hand of the evil one. No less than physical illness, demon possession, or occultic manifestations, human opposition reflects the hostility of Satan, determined to crush the fledgling church.[353]

Attacks on the Messenger

Satan did not reserve his anger for those who formerly worshipped him but now sought their freedom. Though the attack took different forms, he also assaulted the source of the problems, Fraser himself.

The nature of the harassment shifted as his ministry progressed. In the early stages, it tended more toward temptation to lethargy in the boring and frustrating tasks of language learning and administration.

Like all new missionaries, unable to communicate sensibly, and facing interminable, excruciating hours of language study alone in his room, Fraser felt his initial enthusiasm draining, and discouragement seeping in to take its place. The danger was laxity, rather than discipline, with noble daydreams of effective ministry at some vague time in the future.

> It is all *if* and *when*. I believe the devil is fond of those conjunctions....
> The Lord bids us work, watch and pray; but Satan suggests, wait until a
> good opportunity for working, watching and praying presents itself –
> and needless to say, this opportunity is always in the future.[354]

A small temptation, perhaps, but laziness leads progressively to life-long failure, and was to be opposed earnestly in disciplined prayer.

In later stages, especially before the breakthrough, the temptation typically took the form of discouragement – even occasionally suicidal despair – over the slow progress and many disappointments of the ministry.

Exhaustion and despondency often left him vulnerable. A day's trip might consist of a descent of 3,000 feet from one village followed by an equally steep ascent to the next, on mountain trails often too treacherous for horse or donkey. Long nights teaching and preaching, coupled with the inadequate diet of the poor mountain tribes, commonly brought him to the edge of exhaustion.

More severe was the disappointment which followed either prolonged periods of apathy on the part of his listeners, or, worse still, renunciation of the faith by those who had only recently converted.

In the fifth year of his ministry, depression set in, and with it, doubt.

> '*Does* God answer prayer?' loomed larger and larger as a tormenting
> question. 'Does He know and care? Your faith, your expectation – what
> is the outcome?' In his solitude, depression such as he had never known
> before closed down upon him. Was he really right in the course he had
> taken? Five years in China, and so little to show for it![355]

Suicidal with despair, Fraser eventually recognised the hand of the evil one at work.

Summary
Fraser demonstrates familiarity with the works of Satan and his minions, but reflects no knowledge of any special class of strategic-level or

territorial demons. His beliefs and experiences consistently correspond with the teaching of Scripture.

Like Jesus and the apostles, he undergoes personal temptation. Like the apostles, he struggles at times with crippling doubt. As in the time of the Gospels and Acts, Satan still manifests his powers in demon possession and in occultic demonstrations. Evil spirits still intimidate their worshippers through the deceptions of mediums and through the harassment of physical illness. Defectors are punished and pressured through persecution.

Satan employs no new weapon against Fraser and the Lisu. Similar strategies are evident in Scripture, and are recorded in the early Church Fathers. In a day when the study of Scripture and of church history is widely neglected, missionary biography may remind Christians of the devil's evil ways. But it would require considerably more evidence to demonstrate that Satan has suddenly changed his tactics or that he has a class of subordinates which the church has overlooked for the last two thousand years.

WAGING WAR AGAINST THE ENEMY

Given the diversity of tactics which Satan employs, it is not surprising that a variety of responses are warranted. In his battle against demonic opposition, Fraser again demonstrates the effectiveness of the strategies employed by Jesus and the apostles. Central to his entire warfare strategy are diligent labour, patient endurance and, above all, persistent prayer.

> The opposition will not be overcome by reasoning or by pleading, but by (chiefly) steady, persistent prayer. The *men* [sic] need not be dealt with (it is a heart-breaking job, trying to deal with a Lisu possessed by a spirit of fear) but the powers of darkness need to be fought. I am now setting my face like a flint: if the work seems to fail, then *pray*; if services, etc., fall flat, then *pray still more*; if months slip by with little or no result, then *pray still more and get others to help you.*[356]

Over the next several years, he had occasion to notice the difference prayer made, observing that when he approached people who had received much prayer, half the work seemed already to be done, by an invisible hand.[357]

Comrades in Arms

To help him in this work, Fraser sought prayer partners among his homeside supporters. Prayer is the key to progress in evangelism and discipleship, he reasoned, and there is no need to be on site for prayer to be effective.[358]

> I should very, very much like a wider circle of intercessors.
>   Our work among the Lisu is not going to be a bed of roses, spiritually. I know enough about Satan to realise that he will have all his weapons ready for determined opposition. He would be a missionary simpleton who expected plain sailing in *any* work of God. I will not, by God's grace, let anything deter me from going straight ahead in the path to which He leads, but I shall feel greatly strengthened if I know of a definite company of pray-ers holding me up.[359]

Writing in the aftermath of World War I, he invoked a military analogy to explain their comparative roles: he would function as an intelligence officer, supplying detailed information concerning the local situation; they would be field officers, leading the charge against the powers of darkness.[360]

Prayer would do what man could not. Again recalling the battle-fields of World War I, he compared Satanic opposition to the horrible gas attacks. Man can no more defeat Satan than a soldier can kill the vapour which chokes off his breath. Only God can overcome the power of Satan, and this he does in answer to the prayers of his people:

> The breath of God can blow away all those miasmic vapours from the atmosphere of a village, in answer to your prayers. We are not fighting against flesh and blood. You deal with the fundamental issues of this Lisu work when you pray against 'the principalities, the powers, the world-rulers of this darkness, the spiritual hosts of wickedness in the heaven-lies.'[361]

In this way, the work of God can begin long before the preacher arrives, so that the word planted can spring to life quickly.

Resisting the Devil

At the time of deepest despair in his personal battle against depression, Fraser was greatly helped by an article on spiritual warfare from a Christian magazine. Based on James 4:7, the author counselled definite, specific resistance of the evil one based on the cross of Christ.

The passive side of leaving everything to the Lord Jesus as our life, while blessedly true, was not all that was needed just then. Definite resistance on the ground of The Cross was what brought me light.... That cloud of depression dispersed.... The Lord Himself resisted the devil vocally: 'Get thee behind me, Satan!' I, in humble dependence on Him, did the same. I talked to Satan at that time, using the promises of Scripture as weapons. And they worked. Right then, the terrible oppression began to pass away.[362]

Reflecting on the incident, he explained, 'In times of conflict, I still find deliverance through repeating Scripture out loud, appropriate Scripture, brought to mind through the Holy Spirit.'[363]

Of course, this could be overdone. Spiritual weakness and defeat could also result from natural causes: too much isolation, too little physical exertion, neglect of the mental stimulation provided by hard study.[364] On one occasion he reacted strongly to a setback, spending hours in prayer. Reflecting later, he commented, 'I now think that a long healthy walk was indicated, or wholesome Lisu study, rather than the "knee-drill" I practised with such signal failure.'[365] This is no excuse for laxity in prayer; it simply recognises that devotion can lead to obsession if no limits are established.

Prayer for Healing

Through early experiences of new converts reverting to spirit worship, Fraser learned another important lesson. These people, steeped in animism for generations upon generations, still lived in fear of the demons, and took every illness and death as a sign of demonic retaliation.

The only thing many of the people are waiting for is to know whether it is *really safe* to throw the evil spirits overboard and turn to Christ. It is important to pray for those who have already turned Christian, that their faith and constancy may be equal to all tests, and that the Spirit's power for the healing of sickness may be with them. For a man to turn Christian and then be smitten down with sickness, at once discredits the Gospel in the eyes of the Lisu.[366]

Once again safeguards are necessary. Fraser neither expected healing to come whenever the people wanted it, nor did he resist the use of available medicine or other common-sense remedies, such as proper diet. Nevertheless, he found the tribespeople firm believers in divine healing, and for the most part encouraged them in this (though he experienced some reservations about praying for his sick horse or for some new-born pigs!).[367]

Spiritual Warfare

One Christmas Day, near the Burma border, Fraser preached in Middle Village, a hamlet of thirteen families. Deeply disappointed when two village heads influenced the others against becoming Christians, he withdrew to pray. The Lord met him through the record of Jehoshaphat's battle against the Moabites (2 Chron 20:15-17):

> 'Do not be afraid or discouraged because of this vast army. For the battle is not yours, but God's.... You will not have to fight this battle. Take up your positions; stand firm and see the deliverance the Lord will give you.... Do not be afraid; do not be discouraged.'[368]

He spent the afternoon, and then the evening in prayer, until around midnight he recorded in his journal:

> Seem distinctly led to fight against 'principalities and powers' for Middle Village. Have faith for the conversion of that place, and pray as a kind of bugle-call for the hosts of heaven to come down and fight for me against the powers of darkness holding these two old men who are hindering their villages ... from turning to Christ. Have a good time of fighting prayer, then sleep in much peace of mind.[369]

The next morning he retraced his steps. Eleven out of the thirteen families turned to the Lord. 'Victory,' Fraser recorded, 'just as expected – hardly striking a blow!'

Yet there was a supplementary lesson to be learned. Soon after his dramatic victory, he was rebuffed at another village. Withdrawing again for prayer, he claimed the place for Christ. The next day he returned. Still the village was antagonistic; worse yet, even his Lisu helper turned against him and his message. The defeat was painful, but profitable: 'The rebuff of spirit has been very severe,' he wrote in his journal, 'and I shall walk more humbly before the Lord – yes, and before Satan too, after this.'[370]

Overconfidence is to be avoided just as much as a lack of faith. There is no special technique of prayer which, if discovered and properly employed, will guarantee victory over the forces of darkness.

The Sovereignty of God

When God finally worked among the Lisu, he did so in a way which demonstrated his autonomy. Certainly he acted in response to the prayers offered by both Fraser and his supporters. But those prayers neither forced him to respond, nor determined the way in which he would work.

Fortunately Fraser had already learned this lesson through experience.

> I have often in time past given way to depression, which always means spiritual paralysis, and even on this last trip have been much downcast, I admit, over the state of the people.... My mistake has too often been that of too much haste. But it is not the people's way to hurry, nor is it God's way either.[371]

Noticing that Jesus never hurried, nor was ever flustered, he took the Saviour as a model.

> We can afford then to work in the atmosphere of eternity. The rush and bustle of carnal activity breathes a spirit of restlessness: the Holy Spirit breathes a deep calm.... Let us shake off 'dull sloth' on the one hand and feverishness on the other.[372]

He learned to wait patiently for the Lord.

Eventually the Lord did work, but not in the way anyone expected. The hand of the Lord tarried so long, Fraser felt that the time had come to offer for service in another area, where the people were responsive and the missionaries taxed beyond measure by the needs. But first, he decided to make one last trip around the region.[373]

In one village after another the people demonstrated a new openness to the gospel and a willingness to renounce the worship of spirits. One family in the first village; seven more in the following days; ten in another village; fifteen in the next week; five in another; a fitting anniversary celebration of his eight years in China.

The devil fought back, possessing one child and compelling him to throw himself into the fire. But deliverance came in answer to prayer, and the work of God spread. Twenty-four families in one village; forty-nine out of fifty-nine in another. In the end, one hundred and twenty-nine families, six hundred people in all, came to Christ. There was now far too much work to do for Fraser to offer his services elsewhere.

But more, much more, was to come. And it came in surprising fashion: God did more without the missionary than with him. A Lisu convert named Moh spread the gospel throughout the region where he lived. In an area which had rejected the gospel five years earlier, so many were expressing interest in the gospel that Moh sent for Fraser.

Tied down with ministry in his own region, Fraser could not go, but instead sent his only available associate, the newly appointed missionary Allyn Cooke. Despite his inability in the language, Cooke and his two Lisu colleagues led thirty families to Christ in two weeks.

Returning to the base city for further language studies, Cooke left the two Lisu workers behind. Within the next several weeks, scores more families came to Christ through the efforts of these two evangelists. Fraser was not slow to see the hand of God at work.

> Some things especially please me about this new Eastern district. In the first place, the work was practically begun and has been almost wholly carried on by the Lisu themselves, however raw and poorly trained. They have not only passed on the little they know, but have taught others to teach in their turn.... Another matter for thankfulness is that the proportion of Christians to heathen is so large. In some vicinities scarcely any heathen families remain.[374]

In the new district alone, two hundred and forty families had embraced Christ, more than the previous total for the entirety of his ministry.

A total of four hundred households were won within sixteen months. Travelling from village to village Fraser was amazed at the reception given both him and his message.

> They will take you to a village you have never set foot in or even heard of before, and you will find several families of converts there.... They just *want* to be Christians, when they hear all about it, and just turn Christian, missionary or no missionary. Who put that 'want-to' into their hearts? If they are not God's chosen, God's elect, what are they?[375]

The glorious work of God sought for ten years had come in God's timing and in answer to prayer.

CONCLUSION

Thinking back over the long years of sowing and the sudden, bounteous harvest, Fraser reflected, 'I used to think that prayer should have the first place and teaching the second. I now feel it would be truer to give prayer the first, second and third place, and teaching the fourth.'[376]

The lessons of the past are quickly forgotten, and need to be repeated to each new generation, if they are not to be learned all over again through trial and error, and painful experience. From Fraser, and from numerous other missionaries of previous generations, we are reminded that all our methods, techniques, principles, and ministry will ultimately count for naught unless we recover the importance and urgency of fervent, believing, disciplined prayer.

Proponents of SLSW are right at least in this: evangelical ministry is often – though not always nor in all places – insipid and ineffective, and our inconsistency in prayer and timidity in spiritual warfare are major causes of this impotence.

But the solution is not to invent some new techniques, methods, principles, or ministries. As a younger colleague of Fraser commented some twenty-five years ago:

> In a day when new and exciting cutting edges are being recommended, the tendency is to be carried away with new ideas and relegate the traditional trusty weapons to a place of lesser significance or to throw them away altogether.... It is easy and less troublesome to go along with the contemporary mood and give priority to outward means and methods that promise to increase the effectiveness of our service and our praying, but which often do it at the expense of inner reality.[377]

The less dramatic but more reliable solution is to recover what we have lost.

It is time to confess our general apathy for the glory of God and for the salvation of the lost. It is right to repent of our preoccupation with careers, family welfare, leisure activities and material goods. We should open our eyes to see that behind all the disasters which surround us are Satan and myriad evil ones.

Let us learn from J. O. Fraser – and from others like him – to stand firm on the promises of God, to resist the hosts of darkness, to intercede for one another, to pray in detail for the ministry, and to work hard for the glory of God. As Fraser comments: 'Here then we see God's way of success in our work, whatever it may be – a trinity of prayer, faith and patience.'[378]

CONCLUSION

SLSW & EVANGELICAL
MISSIONS STRATEGY

*Summary: SLSW is popular, despite its fundamental errors,
in large measure because its worldview is characteristic
of populist evangelicalism.*

By now the conclusions of this study should be clear. There remains only to tease out a couple of implications. At the risk of labouring the matter, though, perhaps the briefest of summaries is permissible, if for no other purpose than to clear minds made groggy by the long and winding journey.

The evidence cited for SLSW is unconvincing. Scripture provides no support, animism is an unreliable guide, and the 'case study' evidence is anecdotal rather than verified. If arguments were counted rather than weighed, the point might be carried. But the evidence simply does not pass scrutiny. The absence of proof makes it easy to devise exciting hypotheses, but considerably harder to develop convincing ones.

The closest counterparts to the theory of territorial spirits come from intertestamental literature and from medieval theology. The New Testament rejects the former; the Reformation, the latter.

The closest parallels to the practice of warfare prayer come from populist magic, whether in the first-century or during the middle ages. The New Testament rejects the former; the Reformation, the latter.

In the end, it is likely that tutelary spirits exist, and that they are *not* territorial (at least they are not in Scripture, or, for the most part, in animism). Probably some are angelic, and others demonic. Due to spotty and inconsistent evidence, it is not possible to determine how their respective jurisdictions are differentiated.

Warfare prayer is without a shred of support in the Old Testament, and is specifically prohibited in the New (2 Pet. 2:10-12; Jude 8-10). Then again, nothing is lost in rejecting this technique, because we do not need to defeat Satan. Christ has defeated him already, and will one day destroy him. He needs no help, which is certainly a relief, because mortals could provide none if it were necessary. Our role is to proclaim Christ boldly, cast out demons as they manifest, resist temptation at all times, and stand fast in persecution. That gives us all we can handle, and sometimes more.

While SLSW thus has little to commend it, and gives much cause for concern, it should not be characterised as a unique aberration within an otherwise solid and reliable evangelicalism. Those who have resisted this particular digression from Scripture and from the mainstream of Christian tradition must not assume an air of superiority. For much of evangelicalism – even those segments most resolutely opposed to the teachings of SLSW – follows the same methodology and shares a common underlying assumption. These similarities go a long way toward explaining the easy acceptance and rapid spread of SLSW.

Scripture and Novelty

Proponents of SLSW reflect a typical evangelical piety toward Scripture, coupled with a familiar evangelical tendentious appeal to Scripture. Devotion to the Bible is a virtue only when coupled with a concern for the original meaning of the text. Otherwise veneration becomes a guise – albeit unwittingly – under which speculation captivates a credulous Christian public.

We insist that everything we do must be validated by the Bible, even those things never imagined in ancient times. This veneration to the abstract notion of divine revelation (rather than to the concrete revelation of Scripture) is so intense that it often leads to all manner of contortions in the search for proof-texts to endorse everything from aerobics and dieting to management, marketing and psychology.

In such an environment, it comes as no surprise to read that SLSW 'will be of little value for strategizing world evangelisation unless there is some biblical warrant for suggesting it.'[379] Yet this is coupled with statements of purpose, such as:

> In this book I have tried my best to show substantial justification for regarding strategic-level spiritual warfare as the will of God;[380]

> I will present my evidence as cogently as I can;[381]

> My task has now become to produce a book that presents a cogent rationale for the ministry of strategic-level intercession;[382]

> I attempt in this book to justify strategic-level spiritual warfare as one of the legitimate contemporary ministries of the church.[383]

SLSW is a pre-existing practice in search of justification. It finds what it is looking for, or creates what it needs.

Whatever does not appear in the text can be read into it. 'I believe' becomes the new hermeneutic.[384] In the absence of explicit biblical teaching, it is sufficient to offer implications, possibilities, opinions and assumptions.[385] No matter that no commentator supports this interpretation.[386] The same tendentiousness affects the interpretation of history and empirical data.

This approach brings to mind Ben Franklin's quip: 'So convenient a thing is it to be a reasonable creature, since it enables one to find or make a reason for every thing one has a mind to do'.[387] At the same time, this methodology is not unique to SLSW. It is more typical, than atypical, of evangelical innovation as a whole.

Centuries ago Luther warned against artificial appeal to Scripture in promotion of new teachings.

> Woe betide all our teachers and authors, who go their merry way and spew forth whatever is uppermost in their minds, and do not first turn a thought over ten times to be sure it is right in the sight of God! These think the devil is away for a while in Babylon, or asleep at their side like a dog on a cushion. They do not consider that he is round about them with all his venomous flaming darts which he puts into them, such superlatively beautiful thoughts adorned with Scripture that they are unaware of what is happening.[388]

He also commented on the allure of theological speculation:

> We Germans are the kind of fellows who pounce upon anything new and cling to it like fools, and if anyone restrains us, he only makes us more crazy for it; but if no one restrains us, we will soon on our own become fed up and bored with it, and soon chase after something else that is new. Thus the devil has the advantage that no teaching or fancy so clumsy can arise but he can find disciples for it, and the clumsier the more quickly.[389]

Perhaps that temperament is not exclusively German, but universally human.

These warnings need a fresh hearing in a day when Scripture is often used less as a guide to faith than as a source of proof-texts to justify views reached by other means and on other grounds. We need less devotion to the Bible as a talisman, and more respect for it as the revelation of God to be heard and obeyed.

But, of course, tendentiousness is not the monopoly of confessing Christians, whether evangelical or not. It is equally conspicuous in the wider world, even among those much vaunted pursuers of truth, professional academicians. Sociologist Irving Horowitz recently warned against the proclivity among academicians for constructing grand theories.[390]

> The battlefield of ideas is strewn with system builders. For individuals who are convinced that they have a special divination never before seen

on the earth, only grandiose theorising will suffice....

The need to keep pace with changes in ordinary affairs requires that we start with facts and truths and end with ideas and beliefs. To reverse this process, to start with general theory, is but to insure fanaticism. The last temptation of the theorist is to fit reality into his or her model of social life. Once the researcher yields to that temptation, all is lost. Vanity replaces modesty, and the need of the scholar becomes the preservation of 'face' rather than the recognition of our fallibility and finitude.[391]

Creativity, innovation and novelty are prerequisites for academic respectability and advancement. But they often subvert the quest for truth, and cloud the perception of reality.

Rewarding novelty works better in the hard sciences, where technology is constantly advancing. But in theology and missiology, disciplines which rely on the revelation of God in Scripture and his work in history, originality is safe only in much smaller doses. Yet the same pressure exists in Christian as in pagan academia: prestige, fame, and financial reward are largely tied to innovation. And the motivational-lecture circuit is even more insistent on novelty. The development of theology and missiology as academic disciplines, and even more their popularisation on the lecture circuit, should be a boon to the church, but given present trends they are more likely to be a calamity.

God and Technique

In a second respect SLSW mirrors wider evangelicalism, that is, in its use of technique. More than a decade ago, sociologist James Hunter drew attention to the transmogrification of evangelicalism by the forces of modernity.[392] Particularly germane to present concerns is functional rationalisation; or in simpler terms, 'technique'.

'Technique' sprang to life on the factory floor in the early years of industrialisation, but has now spread throughout the entirety of life. Its diverse manifestations share common characteristics:

(1) numerical quantification of success;
(2) the pursuit of efficiency through the application of method;
(3) the rise of the expert to standardise, codify, and train in the application of method.[393]

The primary objection to technique is its application of mechanistic methods to all of life.

Admittedly machines and production lines can be engineered for greater efficiency, lower costs, and a standardised product. But are such methods effective or appropriate in dealing with human beings? Neil Postman groans:

> In the United States, we have experts in how to raise children, how to educate them, how to be loveable, how to make love, how to influence people, how to make friends. There is no aspect of human relations that has not been technicalised and therefore relegated to the control of experts....
>
> I assume I do not need to convince the reader that there are no experts – there can be no experts – in child-rearing and lovemaking and friend-making. All of this is a figment of the Technopolist's imagination.[394]

If such methods are neither effective nor appropriate in dealing with human beings, should they be used to manage God?

The consensus among sociologists is that the rise of technique is a form of secularisation. Theoretical rationalisation denies the existence of God through naturalistic science or rationalistic philosophy. Functional rationalisation manages his power through the application of technique. Either way, the end result is largely the same: God becomes redundant. We have been so preoccupied with the frontal assault by 'secular humanists' that we have been covertly undermined by the engineers of modernity.

Procedures used to increase the productivity of machines on the factory floor are first brought into the front office to increase human efficiency: management science is born. But if workers can be managed on the job, worshippers can be managed in church: revivalism is born. If the conversion of individuals can be managed, so can their organisation into groups: Church Growth is born. If God can be managed, so can Satan: SLSW is born.

Virtually everything evangelicalism now does is quantified numerically, systematised in small steps, codified in booklets, and standardised through training sessions. Witnessing, conversion, discipleship, quiet times, prayer, finding the will of God, receiving the Holy Spirit, speaking in tongues, identifying spiritual gifts, church growth, healing, casting out demons, and evangelising the world by AD 2000: effectiveness in ministry depends on finding and using the right technique.[395] And experts run seminars to provide the requisite training, for a nominal fee considering the powerful insights offered.

So it is perfectly consistent with the worldview of mainstream evangelicalism to describe SLSW as 'spiritual technology for completing the Great Commission in our generation.'[396] Or to warn that 'if we do not use our God-given authority to "bind the strong man" and to neutralise the power of territorial spirits .... the principalities can therefore keep possession of their human trophies and keep whole people groups in spiritual captivity. The choice is ours, not God's.'[397]

Or to claim that SLSW offers missions *the greatest power boost it has had since the time that William Carey went to India in 1793.*'[398]

Technique is equally assumed in the sub-titles of texts promoting SLSW: *How to Seek God's Power and Protection in the Battle to Build His Kingdom;*[399] *How to Use Spiritual Mapping to Make Your Prayers More Strategic, Effective and Targeted.*[400]

Similarly technique comes to expression in the advertised benefits accruing to SLSW. Christians purportedly need to learn 'the language, principles and protocols of the spiritual dimension' so that they can minister more effectively.[401] 'The more skilful we become at spiritual mapping, the more effective we will be.'[402] The use of these methods will 'free the cities and nations of the world from the powers of darkness,'[403] and will 'release Satan's captives into the Kingdom of God.'[404]

Where there is technique, there are experts to codify the necessary procedures, spiritual engineers to ensure that God's power is effectively harnessed and safely applied. There are four 'rules' and one 'law' to change impotent prayer to powerful prayer.[405] Five 'ingredients' make for corporate prayer.[406] Six 'rules' for taking a city.[407] Seven 'principles' of powerful prayer meetings.[408] Ten 'principles' of prayer marches.[409] Another ten 'pitfalls' which may lead to demonic counterattack.[410] Half as many 'musts' for those who want to hear what the Spirit is saying today.[411] A 'master plan' and a 'manual' for spiritual mapping.[412] The list of lists could go on seemingly forever.[413]

That some such technique must exist seems beyond question, given the evangelical mindset. The debate is merely over which technique conveys the Midas touch. Missiologist David Hesselgrave[414] recounts a long list of evangelistic strategies, each initially purporting to be '*the* best way to evangelise the world, proving itself to be *a* way of contributing to that goal, and thus yielding to another method elevated to *the* way': crusade evangelism, 'Evangelism-in-Depth', the Four Spiritual Laws, Evangelism Explosion, the Church Growth Movement, Scripture distribution, home-to-home evangelism, Discipling a Whole

Nation, national evangelists, multi-national teams, the use of mass media.

When each successive technique fails to fulfil its promise, the underlying assumption is rarely questioned. Instead, the neurotic quest continues at an even more frenetic pace. Even now the first hints are emerging that SLSW is on its way out. At least the latest book has shifted the focus of its accolades to what was previously an attendant activity, identificational repentance: 'Of all the forms of prayer I could list, none surpasses the potential of the prayer of identificational repentance for opening the way to spread the gospel.'[415] Though previously 2 Corinthians 10:4 was a proof-text for warfare prayer, it is now a call to engage in identificational repentance.[416]

Hesselgrave cautions against the naivety evident in this never-ending procession of techniques.

> *Let it be crystal clear that this is not written as an indictment of any of these methodologies.... The weakness revealed by this history is not so much that this or that evangelistic method is mistaken and misguided. The weakness is that this or that method is so readily transmuted into an overall strategy for world evangelisation. The weakness is not so much in the method as it is in our penchant for over-simplification and faddishness in embracing one method or partial strategy after another as an 'end-all' strategy.*[417]

But beyond naivety and hubris, a more fundamental and perilous error pervades this entire list: the assumption that there is a key to success, and that it lies in method.

When it is our method that works – whatever that method may be – we have domesticated God (at least in our own imagination). Guinness warns:

> More and more of what was formerly left to God ... is now classified, calculated, and controlled by the systematic application of reason and technique. What counts in the rationalised world is efficiency, predictability, quantifiability, productivity, the substitution of technology for the human, and – from first to last – control over uncertainty.
>
> For religion, the result of rationalisation is what Weber called 'disenchantment'.... All the 'magic and mystery' of life is reduced and removed.... Religion that is irrelevant in practice becomes practically irrelevant. There is no need for God, even in his church.[418]

'Spiritual technology'[419] is an oxymoron, whether that technology is 'conservative evangelical' or 'Third-Wave'.

But we should not need sociology to tell us this. After all, biblical support must be manufactured not simply because the proffered techniques are new, but because the entire mentality of technique is at odds with Scripture. Neither Jesus in the Gospels nor the disciples in Acts follow a systematic or consistent method in ministry. Nor do the epistles ever offer a – let alone 'the' – key to effective ministry. Given that technique reflects a particular worldview, it reflects a worldview at odds with Scripture.

But given that evangelicalism and SLSW share this unbiblical worldview, why does the former show considerable resistance to the latter? Largely because of a shift in paradigm.

As post-modernity supplants modernity, objectivity gives way to subjectivity, rationalism to emotionalism, scientism to spiritism, and mechanism to shamanism.[420] In concrete terms, just as the Church Growth Movement was a manifestation of modernity's mechanistic worldview, so SLSW is an embodiment of post-modernity's spiritistic worldview.[421] A well-intentioned attempt to correct one error has directly precipitated another, because though the paradigm changes, the worldview remains the same.

Thus, Church Growth, 'power evangelism' and SLSW have each, in turn, been promoted as a 'method that works.'[422] Even the same quote from Wesley is used first to endorse Church Growth[423] and then to endorse SLSW.[424] The worldview does not change, only the paradigm does. The chief difference is that conformity to the mechanistic technique of modernity is being replaced by conformity to the spiritistic technique of post-modernity.

In short, those who are alarmed by the tendentious use of Scripture, history and experience in defence of SLSW must be alert to the same tendencies within their own traditions. Those who oppose the spiritism of post-modernist, 'Third-Wave' technique are obliged to oppose the mechanism of modernist, evangelical technique.

References

For book titles, refer to bibliography on pages 175-186.

1. Peretti's novels (1986, 1989) have been the stimulus to much of the current interest in demons. His theory of the demonic, however, does not seem to endorse either the concept of territoriality or the distinctive practices of warfare prayer. Consequently, though the theology underlying his novels needs to be elucidated and evaluated, it does not receive much attention here. For a critique, see Guelich 1991, or more briefly, Garrett 1995: 190-95.

2. Wagner 1993a: 25.

3. Wagner 1990: 90; 1992: 133.

4. Wagner 1993a: 11.

5. Wagner 1996: 46 emphasis in original.

6. Wagner 1992: 166.

7. Wagner 1993a: 20; cf. 1996: 32-33.

8. For example, Reddin 1989: 211-12; Wimber 1990: 183-92; Pawson 1992: 68-70; Robb 1993: 173-84; Hagin 1993: 171-249; Kopfermann 1994.

9. Wagner 1993a: 19; 1996: 13-14.

10. To the best of my knowledge, there has not yet been a comprehensive response in English. The two most extensive analyses that I have found are Taylor (1993) and Kopfermann (1994). The former is detailed, but is limited in scope to the concept of territoriality. The latter is broader, though still not comprehensive, and it is available only in German. Other critiques cited in the text above generally devote only a single chapter to the issue.

11. Page (1995) provides a reasonably comprehensive treatment of several of these themes.

12. Wagner 1991a: 20; 1992: 16-19; 1996: 21-22; 1997: 61.

13. Wagner 1992: 18, 76-77; 1996: 21-22.

14. Wagner 1996: 115-116.

15. Wagner 1992: 67-69, 88-89, 94; 1996: 123, 175-77, 192-93, 202, 216; citing Garrett 1989.

16. Wagner 1996: 51, 100-06, 114-16, 220-22, 228, 230, 245; citing MacMullen 1984.

17. Wagner 1996: 175-77, 191, 195-97.

18. Wagner 1996: 191 emphasis added.

19. Wagner 1996: 175-77.

20. Wagner 1996: 195-97.

21. Wagner 1996: 195.

22. Wagner 1996: 212-13.

23. Wagner 1996: 216-17.

24. Wagner 1996: 163, 171, 175, 177, 191, 193, 196, 203.

25. Wagner 1996: 135, 171, 216.

26. Sterk 1991: 150, 161; cf. Wagner 1990: 77, 79.

27. Wagner 1991.

28. Otis 1993: 35.

29. Wagner 1990: 76-79, 85; 1992: 13, 65, 161-62; Sterk 1991: 152, 154, 162.

30. Wagner 1990: 81.

31. Wagner 1990: 81.

32. Wagner 1992: 99-100.

33. Jacobs 1993: 89; cf. Caballeros 1993: 130, 137-39; Lorenzo 1993: 117; Lawson 1991: 37, 39.

34. Wagner 1993a: 14.

35. Wagner 1993c: 224.

36. Wagner 1993d: 144-45, 216-20.

37. Wagner 1992: 163-66.

38. Wagner 1993b: 56; cf. 1990: 78; 1992: 176; 1991b: 43; 1996: 21-22, 150, 152.

39. Wagner 1991b: 43.

40. Otis 1993: 35; Sterk 1991: 150.

41. Wagner 1992: 77, 79.

42. Otis 1993: 35, 39; Sterk 1991: 150; Wagner 1990: 76; 1996: 258.

43. Dawson 1991: 139; Wagner 1990: 79; Lawson 1991: 37; Sterk 1991: 154.

44. Wagner 1990: 76, 77; 1992: 13; Silvoso 1991: 114; Sterk 1991: 154.

45. Wagner 1990: 82.

46. Wagner 1990: 85.

47. Wagner 1990: 84.

48. Wagner 1990: 77; 1992: 76-77; 1996: 22; Sterk 1991: 151.

49. Wagner 1990: 76; 1992: 62-63; 1996: 150; 1997: 84; Lawson 1991: 35; Sterk 1991: 147-48.

50. Wagner 1990: 76.

51. Wagner 1990: 76; Lawson 1991: 36.

52. Wagner 1992: 77, 79.

53. Sterk 1991: 161.

54. Wagner 1992: 76-77 emphasis added; also 1990: 77; Sterk 1991: 154; cf. Wagner 1996: 22.

55. Wagner 1997: 82.

56. Wagner 1997: 84-85.

57. Wagner 1992: 53.

58. This is another area of ambiguity. While some proponents insist on exact names, Dawson writes, 'Getting the exact name of the demons at any level is not necessary, but it is important to be aware of the specific nature or type of oppression' (1989: 156). In his recent book, Wagner implies that some demons have only functional names and not proper names (1997: 85).

59. Wagner 1992: 63-64, 147-50, 176; 1993a: 18; 1993d: 194; 1997: 85; McGregor and Klopp 1993: 217; Beckett 1993: 155.

60. Wagner 1992: 143-50.

61. Wagner 1993a: 25.

62. Otis 1993: 31-32; cf. Wagner 1997: 96.

63. Jacobs 1993: 81; also McGregor & Klopp 1993: 219; Wagner 1988b: 58; 1993d: 182.

64. Dawson 1989: 140.

65. Wagner 1992:132-40, 163-64. Wagner hastens to add that there is no 'one-to-one cause-and-effect relationship' between the prayers of any individual and the social changes which followed. All he apparently means is that certain individuals prayed specifically for the particular situation, 'and each one testified after a particular season of prayer that they sensed something had been changed in the spiritual realm' (1992: 164). Even with this qualification, the claims are striking.

66. Wagner 1993d: 137; cf. Beckett 1993: 154, 158; Lorenzo 1993: 172.

67. Wagner 1992: 28, 33, 101; 1990: 81.

68. Wagner 1990: 77.

69. Wagner 1996: 21.

70. Wagner 1996: 134; cf. 1996: 21, 22, 36, 228, 258.

71. Wagner 1996: 135. This slant is likely to shape the debate since Wagner has institutionalised it through the United Prayer Track of the AD 2000 and Beyond Movement. Wagner (1996: 249-62) provides a copy of 'The Philosophy of Prayer for World Evangelisation Adopted

by the A.D. 2000 United Prayer Track'. Section 16 pertains to 'Our Sphere of Authority', and quotes Luke 10:19 to establish that SLSW is biblical (1996: 258).

72. Wagner 1996: 136-37 emphasis in original. This may be something of an overstatement, for Wagner (1992: 58) himself warns against engaging Satan in battle, and suggests that only 'spiritual commandos' should engage high-level demons.

73. Wagner 1996: 36, 136, 166, 193, 228, 258.

74. Wagner 1996: 135.

75. Wagner 1996: 34-35, 37, 112-13, 163, 247.

76. Wagner 1996: 163, 193.

77. Wagner 1996: 87, 89, 176, 188 emphasis in original.

78. Wagner 1992: 150-58.

79. Wagner 1992: 130-39.

80. Jacobs 1993: 74; Wagner 1993a: 61; Caballeros 1993: 125; Beckett 1993: 154.

81. For example, Wagner 1996: 30-31.

82. Otis 1993: 35.

83. Wagner 1993a: 19; 1992: 12.

84. Wagner 1992: 90.

85. I owe this observation to Dr. Gordon Wong, lecturer at Trinity Theological College, Singapore.

86. For example, 1 Enoch 9-10; 20:5; 1QM 9:15-16; 1QM 17:6-7; Rev 12:7. Di Lella suggests that this is a survival of an ancient notion that each city-state or nation or empire had a tutelary god as protector (1978: 283; Goldingay 1989: 291; Russell 1989: 118; Collins 1987: 88). Whether or not this is true, what prompts the suggestion is the recognition that the spirits in Daniel 10 are linked with political entities (not with geographical territories). For an extended discussion of guardian angels over nations, see Russell 1964: 235-62.

87. Otis 1993: 35.

88. Warner 1986: 98.

89. Dawson 1989: 149.

90. Wagner 1992: 66 emphasis added.

91. Collins 1987:88.

92. Wagner 1992: 89.

93. see Greenlee 1994.

94. Wagner 1992: 89 emphasis added.

95. Wagner 1992: 89 emphasis added.

96. The entire argument derives from – but misconstrues – an article by missiologist Jacob Loewen (1986). Loewen's thesis is that, 'Many, if not most, tribal and peasant societies *experience* their deities as *tribally, geographically, or functionally* specialised' (1986: 3 emphasis added). He avoids two errors which vitiate SLSW. First, Loewen implicitly distinguishes phenomenology from ontology, and explicitly restricts himself to the former. Secondly, he does not try to subsume all forms of specialisation under 'territoriality', but allows for many types, including ethnic and functional specialisation.

97. Wagner 1992: 89.

98. Wagner 1992: 89-90.

99. Wagner 1992: 91-92 emphasis added.

100. Anderson 1974:82. This is largely true, even with respect to Satan. Meyers and Meyers comment, 'Neither in Job nor in Zechariah [two of the rare OT references to 'Satan'] is the Accuser an independent entity with real power, except that which Yahweh consents to give him' (1987: 184; also Clines 1989: 20).

101. Watts 1985: 326; Oswalt 1986: 453.

102. Di Lella 1978: 283.

103. See, for example, Wagner 1992: 77.

104. For example, Wagner 1992: 98; 1996: 211.

105. Baugh 1995: 20.

106. Contra Wagner 1992: 77; Jacobs 1993: 89.

107. Yamauchi 1980: 41-45.

108. Wagner 1992: 87, 94.

109. Mounce 1977: 148.

110. Bauckham 1993: 17-18, 34.

111. I use this pejorative advisedly. There are many reasons why people become prostitutes, and some prostitutes deserve compassion more than judgement (as, for example, when prostitution results from being sold, kidnapped or beaten into submission). In this instance, though, John is filled with contempt, so 'whore' captures his loathing more accurately than 'prostitute' (even if it is somewhat cruder).

112. Reid suggests something similar: 'The spiritual powers, or "demons", that Israel had understood as standing behind the nations and their gods ... were now conceived as the opponents of Christ and his people' (1993: 948).

113. This should, however, be distinguished from the view of Walter Wink (1984), which reduces Satanic opposition to its structural

manifestation. While Satan works through earthly bureaucracies to harass the Church, this in no way nullifies his personal existence.

114. It should be noted that demon possession is an entirely different topic. Proponents of SLSW specifically distinguish that sort of demon from ruling demons. So this analysis does not discuss exorcism, beyond affirming that *used judiciously*, it remains a vital component of Christian ministry (contra Powlison 1995).

115. Wagner 1992: 57.

116. Wagner 1996: 106-9, 188.

117. Wagner 1992: 66.

118. Keil 1985: 416.

119. Hiebert 1992: 879.

120. Murphy appeals to Daniel to silence critics of new directions in spiritual warfare.

> 'The sudden emergence of strong opposition among some evangelicals to the contemporary attempt to understand the activity of such evil spirits and to guide the people of God into warfare against them puzzles me. Fortunately for Daniel, such opposition either was not forthcoming or was ignored by him' (1992: 523, n15).

Proponents of warfare prayer would presumably meet less opposition if they followed Daniel's example, rather than construing him to be following theirs. Those who are not satisfied with Daniel's caution cannot justifiably invoke him to defend their boldness.

121. Wagner 1991a: 19.

122. Wagner 1997: 83.

123. Wagner 1991a: 19.

124. This work is no longer extant, but the relevant portion can be reconstructed with a reasonable degree of certainty based on Jude 9 and other sources (see Bauckham 1983: 65-76).

125. As Green observes, Jude uses an argument *ad hominem*, without ever indicating whether he views the account as factual or apocryphal (1987: 183).

126. Watson 1988:56. Bauckham contrasts these two interpretations, preferring the latter to the former (1983: 60-62). Yet his view is possible only by minimising the three-fold use of 'slander' (vv 8, 9, 10) as a linguistic catch-word rather than a semantic parallel; (2) translating *tolmao* as 'presume' rather than 'dare'; (3) emphasising the single use of 'presume' over the thrice repeated 'slander'; (4) suggesting that

most interpreters, modern and ancient, have misunderstood the passage; (5) attributing a similar misunderstanding to the author of 2 Peter, who takes over not only the story but also much of the vocabulary, yet misses the point because he is allegedly unfamiliar with the Assumption of Moses.

Bauckham argues that since the Qumran community slanders the devil (see 4Q280-82, 286-87), Jude would not have insisted on showing him respect. But this could just as well be an argument against his interpretation: it illustrates the sort of practice that Jude opposes. Even if Bauckham is right with respect to Jude, he concedes that 2 Peter applies this text to those who slander demons (1983: 262-63).

In any event, one wonders why it is necessary to choose one interpretation or the other. Jude seems to have both in mind. Michael does not slander Satan; he does ask the Lord to rebuke him. From the former, we learn not to vilify the demons; from the latter we learn to turn them over to God.

127. Of course, biblical precedents demonstrate clearly that this prohibition permits exorcism commands, or retorts when under temptation, such as 'Get behind me, Satan' (Mark 8:33; Matt 16:23), provided that these are not accompanied by impudence.

128. Wagner 1996: 228-230.

129. Wagner 1996: 230.

130. Kelly 1969: 338.

131. Wagner 1992: 67. In his recent book, Wagner (1996) finds numerous instances of warfare prayer in the New Testament. But he concedes that many of the accounts 'could conceivably be interpreted as something other than strategic-level spiritual warfare' (p. 163). Among the more implausible suggestions are: (1) unlike James, Peter escaped early martyr-dom because the Church used warfare prayer (pp. 177-178); (2) John Mark deserted the apostolic team because he was intimidated by aggressive confrontation with demons (p. 194); and (3) Paul failed in Athens because the territorial spirits were too deeply entrenched for him to overcome, but instead tricked him into using a faulty evangelistic strategy (pp. 204-207). In the absence of evidence, hypotheses are free, but unconvincing.

Oddly, within a year, Peter's rescue is instead attributed to his having a personal intercessor, thus substantiating the thesis of Wagner's new book (1997: 153). It would appear that biblical silences are pregnant with meaning.

132. Wagner 1996: 209.

133. Wagner 1996: 202.

134. Wagner 1996: 213.

135. Wagner 1996: 213.

136. Wagner 1996: 216-217.

137. For examples, see Betz, ed. 1992.

138. Specialists in ancient magic commonly identify three character-istics which set it off from biblical practice and teaching: (1) a high regard for Hebrew phrases, often misunderstood but viewed as powerful; (2) a stress on the efficacious power of names; and, (3) an emphasis on angels and demons (Charlesworth, ed. 1985: 715; Arnold 1992a: 31). SLSW clearly corresponds to the second and third. Interestingly, Wagner (1992: 149) acknowledges the parallel with first-century magic but considers it an argument in favour of SLSW!

139. Arnold 1992a: 1.

140. Lincoln 1990: 61-62.

141. Similarly, in 3:15 Paul describes God as 'the Father, from whom every family, both in heaven and on earth, derives its name' (author's translation). In first-century parlance, 'families in heaven' would include all spirits, both good and bad. So Paul offers two reasons why Christians do not need to identify the names of the spirits in the effort to gain power over them: Christ has been exalted above all names (1:21); and the Father originally assigned the names (3:15). That is to say, God has always had power over the spirits and in Christ he demonstrated his superiority over them.

142. Arnold 1992a: 73-75.

143. Paul emphasises the close connection between Christ and Christians in his word-choice and in his syntax. He uses compound verbs, and adds the prepositional phrase 'in/with Christ': the Ephesians were 'co-made-alive' 'with Christ'; they were 'co-raised' and 'co-seated-in-the-heavenlies' 'with Christ' (2:5-6).

144. Wright adroitly captures the irony of the cross as the defeat of demons:

> 'These powers, angry at his [Christ's] challenge to their sovereignty, stripped *him* naked, held *him* up to public contempt, and celebrated a triumph over *him*. In one of his most dramatic statements of the paradox of the cross ... [Paul] declares that, on the contrary, on the cross God was stripping *them* naked, was holding *them* up to public contempt, and leading *them* in his own triumphal procession' (1986: 116).

145. Lincoln 1990: 194.

146. Wagner 1992: 190-95.

147. Wagner 1992: 126.

148. Wagner 1992: 126-127.

149. See, for example, *Encyclopædia Britannica* 1988, s.v. 'Emancipation Proclamation.'

150. A similar problem arises with the more common analogy of D-Day and V-E Day, originally suggested by German New Testament scholar Oscar Cullmann (1951: 84-88). This analogy is certainly more appropriate, in that D-Day was not a toothless document but actually achieved something. Yet there is a huge difference between securing a beachhead and defeating an enemy. The crucifixion and resurrection of Jesus signifies more than a victory in the initial battle of a long campaign. It marks the decisive defeat of Satan.

151. Wright 1986: 114; see also Bruce 1984: 27-28.

152. Otis 1993: 31-32; Wagner 1996: 30, 46. Otis gives two reasons why demonic opposition is stronger now than ever before: 'demonic entrenchment' and 'the lateness of the hour'. The latter misinterprets Rev 12:2 as a reference to our time in particular; the original reference was to the entire age following the resurrection of Christ and including our time. The former assumes that the longer demons control an area, the stronger their power is. But to suggest that demons have always controlled the countries of the 10/40 window is to run roughshod over the history of the Church. Within the first five centuries of this era, the Church had spread throughout much of what is now the Muslim world (including North Africa, Egypt, Syria and Persia), and also into India. Within the next two centuries the gospel had spread all along the 'silk routes' into China. (For this quick survey I am indebted to Dr. Dan Bloomquist, lecturer in missions at Singapore Bible College.)

153. Wink 1984: 86-88.

154. Lincoln 1990: 431.

155. Lincoln 1990: 442.

156. Wagner 1992: 123.

157. Undeniably Christians are called 'to advance' the kingdom of God through evangelism and missions (Arnold 1992b: 156-59; Warner 1986: 91-92). But such an idea is not expressed – in the nature of the case it cannot be expressed – by the use of 'stand'. Nor are these activities portrayed in Scripture as assaults on Satan.

158. Balz 1993a: 10; Oepke and Kuhn 1967: 295.

159. Lincoln 1990: 442.

160. Lincoln 1990: 442-43.

161. Wagner 1993d: 134-35.

162. Wagner 1997: 154.

163. Wagner 1992: 58.

164. Wagner 1992: 60; 1996: 142-59; 1997: 67-70.

165. This is a striking example of what biblical scholars call 'illegitimate totality transfer' (Barr 1961: 218-22; Carson 1984: 62). The basic point is that the meaning of any word, phrase or sentence must be explicable in terms of its own context. In short, we learn what John means in Revelation by reading Revelation, not by jumping across to other words in other contexts in other books by other authors.

166. Readers familiar with the legitimate use of word studies will discern immediately that my interest is actually less in the meaning and use of *nikao* than in the concept of spiritual warfare (for the distinction, see Black 1988: 123-24). Thus passages which speak of spiritual warfare without using this particular term are also relevant to the discussion, and passages which use the term without referring to the concept are not. But due to space constraints, I use the word as a window on the concept. A survey of Revelation will reveal that this procedure does not lead to a skewing of the data, in this instance at least.

167. Mounce 1977: 90; Beasley-Murray 1974: 79; Wall 1991: 71.

168. Schürer 1979: 525-29; Hengel 1989: 271-312.

169. Morris 1987: 157.

170. Wagner 1992: 19.

171. Hiebert 1992: 879.

172. Boring notes that in this way John reverses the apocalyptic tradition. In apocalyptic (such as in Daniel), the events in heaven are the cause for those on earth. Here God works on earth through Christ, and this results in the defeat of the evil powers in heaven (1989: 159; Beasley-Murray 1974: 196).

173. This answers a persistent question arising both from the Gospels and from Paul's writings. If the crucifixion, resurrection, and ascension mark the victory of Christ and the defeat of Satan, how is it that spiritual warfare and exorcism are still necessary? Quite simply, Revelation 12 explains, because the defeat of Satan at the cross entails his expulsion from heaven, and anticipates – but does not yet entail – his confinement in hell.

174. Bauckham 1993: 90.

175. Bauckham 1993: 90-91.

176. Boring 1989: 159.

177. Morris 1987: 151.

178. Contra Wagner 1996: 48.

179. Hiebert 1992: 879.

180. I owe the thrust of this section to my former colleague and long-time friend, Rev. Ray Haverfield of Melbourne, Australia.

181. Wagner 1992: 63; 1993a: 14; Otis 1993: 32.

182. Ladd 1972: 171.

183. Morris 1987: 158.

184. Wagner 1993a: 20; cf. 1996: 32-33.

185. Rogers 1983: 92.

186. Rogers 1983: 99.

187. Russell 1964: 240.

188. The reference is to Tobit 3:8, and appears in McGregor and Klopp (1993: 218) and Wagner (1992: 146). Because of space constraints I do not examine this passage in the main text. Briefly, though, Tobit records the names of one angel and one demon, and assumes a two-tier hierarchy (angels and archangels). At the same time, neither the angel nor the demon are territorial, no one either seeks or uses the name of the demon or the angel, and all prayers are directed toward God, not against demons. The account also reflects some magical ideas, such as exorcism through the burning of fish organs.

189. For further introduction to this body of literature, see Nickelsburg 1981; Cohen 1987; Russell 1964; Surburg 1975. The texts are helpfully collected, with English translation, in Charlesworth 1983, 1985 (all quotations below come from this work). Russell (1977: 185-220) provides a useful overview of the intertestamental teachings about Satan and demons.

190. Other works in the intertestamental literature which develop this story include Jubilees (5:1-11; 10:1-14), 2 Baruch (56:12-15), Testament of Reuben (5:6), and Sirach (16:7). The Qumran community also retold the story (CD 2:14-3:13), as did the rabbis (for references, see Aune 1979: 922).

191. A likely reference to national guardian spirits comes in Jub 15:31-32:

'[There are] many nations and many people, and they all belong to him, but over all of them he causes spirits to rule so that they might lead them astray from following him. But over Israel he did not cause any angel or spirit to rule because he alone is their ruler.'

As Russell suggests, this passage may reflect Deut 32:8-9 (1964: 248).

192. To be comprehensive, a survey would have to consider Philo, Josephus, the Qumran scrolls, and possibly early rabbinic writings. My objective, however, is to be illustrative and representative. For brief overviews of the demonology in this literature as a whole, see Bowman 1962: 132-33; Newsom 1992: 249-53; Wilson 1979: 124-27; Aune 1979: 919-23.

193. Josephus, the first-century Jewish historian, recounts Solomon's reputation for healing and exorcism, and the use of his name in later rituals (*Ant* 8.2.5). Duling provides a fascinating account of these ancient traditions concerning Solomon (1983: 944-51).

194. The Testament of Solomon dates somewhere between the first and third centuries AD. On the other hand, there is wide agreement that much of its teaching reflects first-century Palestinian Judaism (Duling 1983: 942). So it sheds light on one sort of demonology which thrived at the time the apostle Paul was ministering.

195. While no contemporary author endorses what the demons report in this text, there are many today who conduct similar interviews (for example, Murphy 1992: 30-31). This practice was also known in the medieval period (see Weyer, 1991 [1563] 359-475). The obvious question is whether it is possible to trust the 'father of lies' to tell the truth; at least Jesus did not (Matt 4:6; Luke 4:10-11). It should also be noted that neither Jesus nor the apostles ever needs to interview demons or uses information gained from a demon.

196. The Testament of Solomon does not actually address its readers directly, but, as Surburg notes (1975: 61), it is a reasonable inference that the author includes all these names for his readers to use in their own dealings with the demonic.

197. Praying to angels for help is not unique to the Testament of Solomon. Commenting on the intertestamental literature in general, Surburg notes, 'That men will utilise the resources available in the form of angelic help is taken for granted' (1975: 61).

This practice is also known among a few of those who practice SLSW today. Lorenzo describes pastors praying two by two, with the first breaking the power of the demon, and the second calling forth the 'opposite spirit' and God's redemptive gift (1993: 191). Similarly,

Caballeros promises that through the practice of SLSW, millions of angels come to man's assistance (1993: 125; cf. Dawson 1989: 140).

198 and 199. Arnold 1992b: 98-99. Arnold actually lists these as five points, and in a different order. I have rearranged them to correspond to the six basic tenets of SLSW. These cha...ges do not affect the substance of his comment.

200. Surprisingly, though several advocates of SLSW show familiarity with Arnold's works and acknowledge his expertise, none challenges – or incorporates – his conclusions (see, for example, Jacobs 1993: 79; Wagner 1992: 68, 97-98, 123, 149).

201. See, for example, Wagner 1996: 100-116.

202. For brief but helpful surveys, see Studer 1992: 226-27; Ferguson 1990: 260-61.

203. For the less accessible works, I rely on Jurgens 1979. References to this work are indicated as follows: Jurgens vol.page item #.

204. Jurgens 3.248 #2161.

205. Pseudo-Dionysius *Celestial Hierarchy* 9.4.

206. John Damascene *Source* 3.2.3, Jurgens 3.334 #2354; also Clement *Miscellanies* 6.17.157.4, Jurgens 1.184 #430.

207. Hiliary of Poitiers *Psalms* 129.7, Jurgens 1.387 #895; also Origen, *Principles* 1.8.1, 2.10.7.

208. See Basil (330-379), *Eunomius* 3.1, Jurgens 2.14 #940; Jerome (347-419), *Matthew* 3.18.10, Jurgens 2.202 #1387; Origen, *Luke* 12, Jurgens 1.201 #475; also Gregory of Nyssa, *Life* 2, Jurgens 2.45 #1022.

209. Aquinas *Summa Theologica* 113.8.

210. Weyer also records pagan belief in demons of islands, mountains, springs, territories, local sites, and households (1991 [1563]: 12). While one or two of these might be geographical, there is no justification for accepting the little evidence which fits this theory and rejecting the bulk of the data. So if we endorse the concept of geographical spirits, we must also accept a wide variety of other specialisations. Weyer describes the various types of jurisdiction generically as 'ancestral tutelary gods with specialised associations', and rejects it all as paganism.

211. Aquinas *Summa Theologica* 110.1.

212. Tertullian *Apology* 22.4, Jurgens 1.115 #278.

213. Aquinas *Summa Theologica* 113.6.

214. Theodoret *Interpretation of Daniel*, Jurgens 3.248 #2161; Aquinas *Summa Theologica* 113.3.

215. Thomas 1973: 29-30.

216. Thomas 1973: 30.

217. Thomas 1973: 30-57.

218. Thomas 1973: 58-89.

219. Origen *Principles* 1.8.1.

220. Justin Martyr *Apology* 5, Jurgens 1.50-51 #112a.

221. Origen *Contra Celsus* 1.6.

222. Augustine *City of God* 10.22.

223. Origen *Contra Celsus* 8.44.

224. Origen *Contra Celsus* 8.27.

225. Origen *Contra Celsus* 8.34.

226. Chrysostom *Homily* 1.6.

227. Augustine *City of God* 10.21.

228. Pseudo-Dionysius *Celestial Hierarchy* 6-10. For a summary of the demonology of Pseudo-Dionysius, see Louth 1989: 35-37; MacGregor 1988: 76.

229. Pseudo-Dionysius, *Celestial Hierarchy* 6-10; cf. John Damascene (645-749), *Source* 3.2.3, Jurgens 2.335 #2355.

230. Gregory the Great (540-604), *Homily* 2.34.7, Jurgens 3.324 #2335. Russell (1984: 94 n6) erroneously attributes this list to Pseudo-Dionysius, and Pseudo-Dionysius' scheme to Gregory the Great. I have followed Aquinas' summary (*Summa Theologica* 108.6); see also Jurgens 2.234 #2355.

231. Cyril of Jerusalem (315-386), *Catechetical Lectures* 23.6, Jurgens 1.362 #849.

232. Gregory of Nazianz (330-389), *Orations* 28.31, Jurgens 2.31 #989.

233. Basil the Great (330-379), *Holy Spirit* 16.38, Jurgens 2.17 #949.

234. Jerome (347-419), *Apology* 1.23, Jurgens 2.205 #1394.

235. Augustine (354-430), *Orosius* 11.14, Jurgens 3.115 #1805. For yet more lists, see Louth 1989: 36. While the lists provided here are of angels, rather than demons, Weyer (1991 [1563]: 78-79) notes that some medieval theologians argued by analogy for nine levels of demons. Others, however, divided them into four elements (demons of fire, air, water, earth) or into compass directions (demons of the East, West, South, North), or into ecological classes (forest-spirits, mountain-spirits, field-spirits, house-spirits), and more. Weyer rejects such speculation as magic and false teaching opposed to holy doctrine and the Christian faith.

236. See Jurgens 2.92 #1125; 2.102 #1148; 2.132 #1239a; 2.159 #1290a.

237. Gregory of Nazianz *Orations* 28.31, Jurgens 2.31 #989.

238. Augustine *Enchiridion* 58.

239. Wagner 1992: 62-63 cf. 1990: 76; 1991: 17, 20; 1996: 235; 1997: 84. If this is the rationale for Satan using demons as his messengers, one wonders what explanation would be offered for God using angels!

240. Aquinas *Summa Theologica* 52.2.

241. Aquinas *Summa Theologica* 52.1-53.3.

242. Anyone who enjoys the speculation of SLSW will gain even more pleasure from the medieval Fathers. In addition to spirit hierarchies, names, ruling function, and presence, Aquinas also discusses their knowledge, will, creation, conversion, fall, punishment, influence, language, and functions (*Summa Theologica* 52-64, 106-114).

243. Thomas 1973: 29-72.

244. Wagner 1996: 92-94 emphasis original.

245. Wagner 1996: 94.

246. Wagner 1996: 101.

247. MacMullen 1984: 108.

248. Wagner 1996: 115-16.

249. Origen *Principles* 1.5.4.

250. *LW* 36.109.

251. *LW* 54.22,112.

252. *Table Talk* CXVIII, cited from Kerr 1943: 28.

253. *Table Talk* LXVII, cited from Kerr 1943: 28.

254. *LW* 54.78.

255. *LW* 54.83.

256. Althaus 1963: 162; cf. Carlson 1948: 49.

257. *LW* 13.17.

258. *LW* 13.97.

259. *LW* 26.282.

260. *LW* 54.105-6.

261. *LW* 54.279-80.

262. *LW* 54.318.

263. *LW* 37.133.

264. *LW* 51.205.

265. Wagner dismisses theological debate as futile: rarely do such discussions cause proponents to change their minds; more commonly

people merely harden their positions (1993d: 211). Luther views the matter differently:

> 'I shall once more set myself against the devil and his fanatics, not for their sake, but for the sake of the weak and simple. For I have no hope that the teachers of a heresy or fanaticism will be converted. Indeed, if that were possible, so much has already been written that they would have been converted' (*LW* 37.19-20).

Besides, who is responsible for any hardening of positions: the one who questions the teaching, or the one who refuses to consider the possibility of correction?

266. *Institutes* 1.14.4.
267. *Institutes* 1.14.4.
268. *Institutes* 1.14.7.
269. *Institutes* 1.14.8.
270. *Institutes* 1.14.17.
271. *Institutes* 1.14.13.
272. *Institutes* 1.14.15.
273. Calvin 1974: 221.
274. *Institutes* 1.14.17.
275. *Works* 6.370-71.
276. *Works* 6.371-79.
277. *Works* 6.373.
278. *Works* 6.374.
279. *Works* 6.375.
280. *Works* 6.379-80.
281. *LW* 54.97.
282. Wagner 1991a: 15-17; 1996: 52-55; 1997: 35-54.
283. A fourth criticism arises from the appeal to Greek to justify the distinction between revelation in Scripture (*logos*) and ongoing personal revelation (*rhema*) (for example, Wagner 1991a: 15-17; 1996: 52-55, 62, 64, 155). There is much to be said for the distinction between these two concepts. But the attempt to construct an aura of credibility by appeal to Greek is unnecessary, and the proposed distinction between these two Greek words is as wrong as it is common.
284. For example, Wimber 1990; Pawson 1992; Robb 1993; Hagin 1993; Kopfermann 1994.
285. McConnell 1988: 189-90.
286. Sterk 1991: 150. Wagner describes this article as 'one of the

finest case studies of spiritual territoriality in a field missionary setting'
(1992: 100).

287. Sterk 1991: 151. Animism is also cited in support of warfare
prayer (or, at least, in support of naming and addressing the spirits)
(Sterk 1991: 158-59). It can happily be agreed that animists assign
names to their deities and that they use these names in appealing for
favours. But what must be demonstrated is that use of the names is
thought to provide the worshipper power over the spirits. In animism,
influence over the spirits is commonly restricted to powerful shaman,
and requires more than possession of spirit names. Since the case for
warfare prayer has not been made from animism, it need not be re-
futed.

288. Wee 1977: 142-181. I am indebted to Elder Chong Ser Choon
of Singapore for reviewing this material.

289. Vogt 1970: 4-16.

290. Sterk 1991: 149-51.

291. Spiro 1967: 43-54. I am indebted to Pastor Kan Myint of
Yangon, Myanmar, for reviewing this material.

292. Geertz 1960:16-28; Koentjaraningrat, 1989: 336-43. Javanese
animism also provides support for the practice of warfare prayer (at
least for interviewing demons in search of their names). When someone comes under spirit possession, a shaman (*dukun*) inquires of the
indwelling spirit: 'What is your name? Where is your home? Why have
you come here? What do you want?' The demon might answer, 'My
name is Kijaji Bendok. My home is on the bridge in front of the market. I came here to eat and drink.' This sort of spirit commonly agrees
to depart once its needs are met (Geertz 1960: 20).

293. Similarly, Ranger describes a variety of overlapping networks
in pre-colonial Africa:

'A hypothetical man in pre-colonial southern Africa could belong suc-
cessively, or even simultaneously, to all those overlapping networks of
religious relationship: for example, he could express his control of his
household through a localised ancestral cult, carry tribute to a distant
territorial shrine, belong to a gun-hunter's guild, and be an initiate of a
spirit possession cult that linked him to men and women who lived along
a trading route. The various cultic layers ... did not fit neatly together to
form a single collective religion' (1993: 74).

That is to say, in African folk religion, some deities were considered geographical, but others were ancestral, functional, or cultic. It is tendentious to cite one type while ignoring the many others.

294. Burnett 1988: 11.

295. Hiebert 1982: 43.

296. Hiebert 1982: 46.

297. Hiebert 1982: 46; 1994: 200; cf. Erickson 1993: 169-71; Priest, Campbell and Mullen 1995.

298. The ideas in this section are not new; they are commonplace in the Christian literature discussing animism (see, for example, Burnett 1988: 245, 247; 1992: 61-62; van Rheenen 1991: 95, 125). Unhappily, such ideas have not received the attention they deserve in recent exhortations for a paradigm shift in evangelicalism. It is one matter to argue for the inadequacy of an existing paradigm. It is something else altogether to offer a comprehensive and superior alternative.

299. Hiebert 1989: 117. Wee remarks similarly that Chinese religion is primarily concerned with the utilisation of power – both secular and religious – rather than with the acquisition of truth (1977: 63-64).

300. See, for example, Spiro 1967: 157-245; Thompson 1979: 31-33.

301. Redfield 1941: xix.

302. Redfield 1956:70. It should be noted that both 'high' and 'low' traditions find place in theology for demons. The major difference is that the 'high' traditions tend to centre on worship of a sovereign deity and expect him to act against the spirits, while the 'low' traditions generally focus on the spirits and devise methods by which people can control them.

303. Priest, Campbell and Mullen 1995.

304. Wagner 1992: 20, 28; 1996: 47.

305. Wagner 1996: 46 emphasis in original.

306. Wagner 1992: 163-64.

307. Wagner 1992: 21; also 13, 25, 37.

308. Wagner 1992: 25-26.

309. Wagner 1992: 38; Hull 1992.

310. Sjöberg 1993: 116.

311. Warner 1991a: 52-53; 1991b: 136-37; Wagner 1988a: 201-2; 1988b: 60-61; 1990: 92; 1991b: 47-48.

312. Priest, Campbell and Mullen have recently tracked down this story. They found that the incident occurred almost fifty years ago, and involved only a few people, during a single afternoon, in a town since forgotten (1995: 40). So even once the source has been tracked

down, several aspects of the report and its interpretation prove impossible to confirm.

313. Sjöberg 1993: 113.

314. Broderick 1952: 285.

315. Hunt, Lee, Roxborogh 1992.

316. Schurhammer 1980: 50-51, n. 402.

317. Schurhammer 1982: 604-5, 608-9, n38; also Steward 1917: 327; Teixeira 1961: 351-54.

318. Schurhammer 1980: 50-51. The nearest I could find to a curse was the statement remembered by one Manoel Mendez Raposo that, 'God will see to it that the land would get what it deserved' (Noonan 1965: 143); or that 'a great trouble would come over the city' (Schurhammer 1980: 50). This, however, was in his farewell sermon, prior to his departure, in church, not at the beach. Moreover, it amounts to nothing more than a warning that God punishes sin. Since Scripture teaches this very truth, such a warning is unlikely to be annulled by spiritual warfare, though it could be made redundant by repentance.

319. Thus I am obviously more cautious than Peter Wagner, who writes: 'My current position is that unless I have special reason not to believe it, I take the testimonies of sincere, lucid people at face value' (1988a: 242).

320. For other illustrations of unreliable data collection and interpretation, see Priest, Campbell and Mullen 1995: 36-40.

321. Wagner 1990: 80.

322. Wagner 1992: 13, 16, 156.

323. Read 1965: 208, 221.

324. Martin 1990: 5, 50-51, 60, 319; Read, Monterroso and Johnson 1969: 51-58.

325. Wagner 1992: 25.

326. Wagner 1992: 23-24.

327. Wagner 1992: 28-33.

328. Wagner 1986: 13; 1973a. These are reminiscent of the conclusions reached earlier by Enns and based on the Argentine experience (1971), and those derived still earlier by Read from the growth of the Brazilian church (1965). More recently these factors have been reaffirmed by Berg and Pretiz (1992), who also pay more attention to the sorts of social, cultural, and structural issues which SLSW and Church Growth analyses both tend to overlook.

329. Wagner 1973a: 29, 33.

330. Wagner 1986: 15, 31, 40-42.

331. Wagner 1992: 26.

332. Wagner 1993b: 57 emphasis original; also 1992: 63, 151; 1993a: 7; Otis 1991: 85; 1993: 32.

333. The literature is vast. Among the best that I have read are Martin (1990) on Latin America; Willis (1977) on Indonesia; Whiteman (1983) on Melanesia; and, more briefly, Hefner (1993) on Java.

334. Sociologist Ronald Johnstone notes the limitations and benefits of social science:

> 'We cannot, for example, determine whether a particular individual's conversion is in fact a personal experience with God Himself in which the Holy Spirit enters the person and leads him or her to certain convictions. We can, however, provide some sociological insight into the context within which conversions occur, point out that conversion is not wholly a psychological phenomenon, and note that it does not occur in a wholly religious context as distinct from a social one' (1992: 73).

If nothing else, this additional insight helps evangelists and missionaries to evaluate the response that does occur, lest a largely social response be received as religious conversion. It also helps to distinguish peoples more likely to be amenable to evangelism from those more likely to be resistant, thus aiding strategy and deployment.

335. Johnstone 1992: 73.

336. Willis 1977: 194.

337. Willis 1977: 210. For similar conclusions based on the spread of the gospel through various regions of the world, see Nida 1974: 83, and Hesselgrave 1978: 304; as well as Read 1969: 247, 255 (Latin America); Whiteman 1993: 184 (Melanesia); Keyes 1993 (Thailand); Hefner 1993 (Java); Brown 1994 (Korea); McKinney 1994 (the Bajju of Nigeria); Berg and Pretiz 1992 (also Latin America); and Elkins 1994 (tribal groups in Mindanao, Philippines).

338. Willis 1977: 196.

339. Wagner 1992: 23.

340. Wagner 1992: 23-24.

341. Martin 1990: 280 emphasis in original.

342. Martin 1993: 116-17.

343. Martin 1990: 258.

344. Martin 1990: 204.

345. Martin 1990: 83.

346. Berg and Pretiz 1992: 115-23.

347. Taylor 1944: 29.

348. Crossman 1982: 36. To prevent a misreading of this text as though it supports SLSW, perhaps it is necessary to state the obvious: while Crossman uses the word 'territory' and speaks of the mountains as 'the stronghold of Satan', she is using these in a general sense, not in the technical sense recently developed by SLSW.

349. Taylor 1944: 71-72.

350. Taylor 1944: 72-73.

351. Taylor 1944: 79.

352. Taylor 1944: 79.

353. Taylor 1944: 94-97.

354. Taylor 1944: 32.

355. Taylor 1944: 89.

356. Taylor 1944: 130.

357. Taylor 1944: 188.

358. Taylor 1944: 173.

359. Taylor 1944: 87.

360. Taylor 1944: 191.

361. Taylor 1944: 228.

362. Taylor 1944: 91.

363. Taylor 1944: 92; also 131,140-41.

364. Taylor 1944: 135.

365. Taylor 1944: 135.

366. Taylor 1944: 119.

367. Taylor 1944: 164-65.

368. Taylor 1944: 154.

369. Taylor 1944: 155.

370. Taylor 1944: 155.

371. Taylor 1944: 161.

372. Taylor 1944: 163.

373. Taylor 1944: 138-40.

374. Taylor 1944: 197.

375. Taylor 1944: 223.

376. Taylor 1944: 228.

377. Mathews 1972: 41.

378. Taylor 1944: 128.

379. Wagner 1990: 78 cf. 1996: 74.

380. Wagner 1996: 247.

381. Wagner 1996: 164.

382. Wagner 1996: 34.

383. Wagner 1996: 37.

384. Wagner 1996: 162, 163, 164, 186, 190, 191, 196, 208.

385. Wagner 1996: 75, 163, 164, 166, 170, 171, 175, 176, 177, 188, 189, 193, 194, 200, 203, 204, 210, 213; 1997: 86.

386. Wagner 1996: 162-63. For a similar critique of Wagner's works on Acts (1994, 1995a, 1995b), see Peskett 1996: 480-84. Peskett writes: 'I felt that Wagner was not sufficiently interested in Luke's own work, but only in the uses he could make of it. Thus we see in Wagner's books, not a picture of Luke and his work, but of Wagner's mirrored face' (p 482). I would add only that this tendentiousness characterises his use of all sources, not only Scripture, but also secondary literature and empirical data.

387. Franklin 1923: 62.

388. *LW* 37.13-18.

389. *LW* 37.19.

390. Symptomatic of this approach is the 'Third-Wave' argument from worldview. Ironically, those who warn vociferously against the distorting effects of a rationalistic worldview typically give scant attention to the distorting effects of a spiritistic worldview (e.g., Wagner 1996: 49-50, 76-77; Kraft 1989).

The former undeniably blinds people to the supernatural where it legitimately appears. Yet the latter equally causes people to see the supernatural where it does not appear. For all the times that ministry experience in the 'Third-World' is cited against the dangers of rationalism, it can equally be adduced to illustrate the dangers of spiritism.

The argument from worldview does not prove anything. It merely alerts all parties not to exclude any of the evidence out of hand. Conclusions must be based on the evidence, not predetermined by philosophical *a priori*, whether rationalistic or spiritistic.

391. Horowitz 1994: 598.

392. Actually this analysis goes back at least as far as Max Weber (1991 [1923]), is a prominent theme in the writings of Jacques Ellul (1964, 1990) and Peter Berger (1963), and is applied to evangelicalism by Os Guinness (1983, 1992, 1993). What Hunter (1983) adds is the convicting force of innumerable examples from core evangelical practices.

393. Ellul 1964: 19-21; also Berger and Kellner 1972: 121-23.

394. Postman 1993: 88.

395. Hunter 1983: 74-84.

396. Wagner 1996: 96, 91, 30.

397. Wagner 1996: 242-43.

398. Wagner 1996: 46 emphasis in original; cf. Wagner 1997: 97.

399. Wagner 1992.

400. Wagner, ed. 1993.

401. Otis 1993: 32-34.

402. Wagner 1993b: 61.

403. Jacobs 1993: 81.

404. Jacobs 1993: 74.

405. Wagner 1993d: 42, 45-56; updated version, Wagner 1997: 131-36.

406. Wagner 1993d: 113-16.

407. Wagner 1993a: 230-31; 1992: 161-79.

408. Wagner 1993d: 118-24.

409. Wagner 1993d: 160-61.

410. Wagner 1992: 184-95.

411. Wagner 1996: 30-31.

412. Caballeros 1993: 137-44.

413. See also Jacobs 1991: 242-45; Dawson 1989: 163-219.

414. Hesselgrave 1994: 88-89.

415. Wagner 1997: 111.

416. Wagner 1997: 111-12; 1996: 238-39 cf. Wagner 1992: 64-65.

417. Hesselgrave 1994: 88-89 emphasis in original.

418. Guinness 1993: 48-49.

419. Wagner 1996: 91.

420. Veith 1994; Carson 1996; Erickson 1994.

421. Veith's analysis of post-modern spirituality (1994: 191-221) underscores at least three characteristics of SLSW: (1) the appeal to, and similarity with, animism; (2) the appeal to personal conviction in the absence of hard evidence and the casual subjectivity in interpreting Scripture; and, (3) the rejection of criticism as judgmental and sub-Christian. Priest, Campbell and Mullen (1995) develop the first criticism at length.

422. On Church Growth, see Wagner 1984a: 201; 1984b: 160-65; 1973: 147-57. On power evangelism, see Wagner 1988b: 87. On SLSW, see Wagner 1992: 28; 1996: 47.

423. Wagner 1987: 31-32.

424. Wagner 1996: 48.

BIBLIOGRAPHY

Biblical and Intertestamental Texts

Aland, Kurt et al, eds. 1993, *Novum Testamentum Graece*. 27th ed. Stuttgart: Deutsche Bibelstiftung.

Charlesworth, James, ed. 1983, *The Old Testament Pseudepigrapha*. Vol 1. Garden City, NY: Doubleday.

Charlesworth, James, ed. 1985, *The Old Testament Pseudepigrapha*. Vol 2. Garden City, NY: Doubleday.

Rahlfs, Alfred, 1971, *Septuaginta*. Stuttgart: Deutsche Bibelgesellschaft.

Vermes, Geza, 1987, *The Dead Sea Scrolls in English*. London: Penguin.

Church Fathers

Aquinas, Thomas, 1990, *Summa Theologica*. Chicago: Britannica.

Augustine, 1988a, City of God. In *The Nicene and Post-Nicene Fathers of the Christian Church*. P. Schaff, ed. 1.2.xi-511. Reprint. Grand Rapids: Eerdmans.

Augustine, 1988b, Enchiridon. In *The Nicene and Post-Nicene Fathers of the Christian Church*. P. Schaff, ed. 1.3.229-76. Reprint. Grand Rapids: Eerdmans.

Calvin, John, 1957, *Institutes of the Christian Religion*. London: Clarke.

Chrysostom, John, 1988, Homily Against Those Who Say That Demons Govern Human Affairs. In *The Nicene and Post-Nicene Fathers of the Christian Church*. P. Schaff, ed. 1.9.177-86. Reprint. Grand Rapids: Eerdmans.

Jurgens, William, ed. 1979, *The Faith of the Early Fathers*. 3 vols. Collegeville, MN: Liturgical.

Louth, Andrew, 1989, *Denys the Areopagite*. London: Geoffrey Chapman.

Luther, Martin, 1974, *Luther's Works*. J. Pelikan & H. Lehmann, eds. St Louis: Concordia. [abbreviated *LW*]

Origen, 1989a, Contra Celsus. In *Anti-Nicene Fathers*. A. Roberts and J. Donaldson, eds. 4: 395-669. Reprint. Grand Rapids: Eerdmans.

Origen, 1989b, De Principiis. In *Anti-Nicene Fathers*. A. Roberts and J. Donaldson, eds. 4: 395-669. Reprint. Grand Rapids: Eerdmans.

Pseudo-Dionysius, 1987, *The Complete Works*. New York: Paulist.

Wesley, John, 1979, *The Complete Works*. Grand Rapids: Baker. [abbreviated *Works*]

Secondary Sources

Althaus, Paul, 1963, *The Theology of Martin Luther*. Philadelphia: Fortress.

Anderson, A. A., 1974, *Psalms 72-150*. London: Marshall, Morgan & Scott.

Arnold, Clinton, 1992a, *Ephesians: Power and Magic. The Concept of Power in Ephesians in Light of Its Historical Setting*. Grand Rapids: Baker.

Arnold, Clinton, 1992b, *Powers of Darkness: A Thoughtful, Biblical Look at an Urgent Challenge Facing the Church*. Leicester: IVP.

Aune, D. E., 1979, Demon. In *International Standard Bible Encyclopedia*. Geoffrey Bromiley, ed. 1:919-23. Grand Rapids: Eerdmans.

Balz, Horst, 1993a, *Panoplia*. In *Exegetical Dictionary of the New Testament*. Horst Balz and Gerhard Schneider, eds. 3:10. Grand Rapids: Eerdmans.

Balz, Horst, 1993b, *Puthon*. In *Exegetical Dictionary of the New Testament*. Horst Balz and Gerhard Schneider, eds. 3:196. Grand Rapids: Eerdmans.

Barr, James, 1961, *The Semantics of Biblical Language*. London: SCM.

Bauckham, Richard, 1983, *Jude, 2 Peter*. WBC. Waco, TX: Word.

Bauckham, Richard, 1993, *The Theology of the Book of Revelation*. Cambridge: Cambridge University Press.

Baugh, S. M., 1995, A Foreign World: Ephesus in the First Century. *Women in the Church: A Fresh Analysis of 1 Timothy 2:9-15*. A. J. Koestenberger, T. R. Schreiner and H. S. Baldwin, eds. Pp. 13-52. Grand Rapids: Baker.

Beasley-Murray, G. R.,1974, *Revelation*. NCB. London: Marshall, Morgan & Scott.

Beckett, Bob, 1993, Practical Steps Toward Community Deliverance. In *Breaking Strongholds in Your City: How to Use Spiritual Mapping to Make Your Prayers More Strategic, Effective and Targeted*. C. Peter Wagner, ed. Pp. 147-70. Ventura, CA: Regal.

Berg, Clayton, Jr. and Paul Pretiz, 1992, *The Gospel People of Latin America*. Monrovia, CA: MARC.

Berger, Peter, 1963, *Invitation to Sociology*. Harmondsworth: Penguin.

Berger, Peter and Hansfried Kellner, 1972, *Sociology Reinterpreted: An Essay in Method and Vocation*. Harmondsworth: Penguin.

Betz, Hans, ed., 1992, *The Greek Magical Papyri in Translation*. Chicago: University of Chicago Press.

Black, David, 1988, *Linguistics for Students of New Testament Greek*. Grand Rapids: Baker.

Boring, M. Eugene, 1989, *Revelation*. Louisville: John Knox.

Bowman, J. W., 1962, Angel. In *Interpreter's Dictionary of the Bible*. George Buttrick, ed. 1:129-34. Nashville: Abingdon.

Broderick, James, 1952, *Saint Francis Xavier (1506-1552)*. London: Burns & Oates.

Brown, G. Thompson, 1994, Why Has Christianity Grown Faster in Korea Than in China? *Missiology* 22: 77-88.

Burnett, David, 1988, *Unearthly Powers: A Christian Perspective on Primal and Folk Religion*. Eastbourne: MARC.

Burnett, David, 1992, *Clash of Worlds: A Christian's Handbook on Cultures, World Religions, and Evangelism*. Nashville: Thomas Nelson.

Caballeros, Harold, 1993, Defeating the Enemy with the Help of Spiritual Mapping. In *Breaking Strongholds in Your City: How to Use Spiritual Mapping to Make Your Prayers More Strategic, Effective and Targeted*. C. Peter Wagner, ed. Pp. 123-146. Ventura, CA: Regal.

Calvin, John, 1974, *The Epistles of Paul the Apostle to the Galatians, Ephesians, Philippians and Colossians*. Grand Rapids: Eerdmans.

Carlson, Edgar, 1948, *The Reinterpretation of Luther*. Philadelphia: Westminster.

Carson, D. A. 1984, *Exegetical Fallacies*. Grand Rapids: Baker.

Carson, D. A. 1996, *The Gagging of God: Christianity Confronts Pluralism*. Grand Rapids: Zondervan.

Clines, David, 1989, *Job 1-20*. WBC. Waco: Word.

Cohen, Shaye, 1987, *From the Maccabees to the Mishnah*. Philadelphia, PA: Westminster.

Collins, John J., 1987, *Daniel*. Hermeneia. Minneapolis: Fortress.

Crossman, Eileen, 1982, *Mountain Rain*. Kent: OMF.

Cullmann, Oscar, 1951, *Christ and Time*. Philadelphia: Westminster.

Dawson, John, 1989, *Taking Our Cities for God*. Lake Mary, FL: Creation House.

Dawson, John, 1991, Seventh Time Around: Breaking Through a City's Invisible Barriers to the Gospel. In *Engaging the Enemy: How to Fight and Defeat Territorial Spirits*. C. Peter Wagner, ed. Pp. 135-142. Ventura, CA: Regal.

Di Lella, Alexander and Louis Hartman, 1978, *The Book of Daniel: A New Translation with Notes and Commentary*. Garden City, NY: Doubleday.

Duling, D. C., 1983, Testament of Solomon. In *Old Testament Pseudepigrapha*. James Charlesworth, ed. 1: 935-59. Garden City, NY: Doubleday.

Elkins, Richard, 1994, Conversion or Acculturation? A Study of Culture Change and Its Effect on Evangelism in Mindanao Indigenous Societies. *Missiology* 22: 167-76.

Ellul, Jacques, 1964, *The Technological Society*. New York: Vantage.

Ellul, Jacques, 1990, *The Technological Bluff*. Grand Rapids: Eerdmans.

Enns, Arlo, 1971, *Man, Milieu & Mission in Argentina*. Grand Rapids: Eerdmans.

Erickson, Millard, 1993, *The Evangelical Mind & Heart: Perspectives on Theological and Practical Issues*. Grand Rapids: Baker.

Erickson, Millard, 1994, *Where is Theology Going? Issues and Perspectives on the Future of Theology*. Grand Rapids: Baker.

Ferguson, Everett, 1990, Demons. *Encyclopedia of Early Christianity*. Everett Ferguson, ed. Pp. 259-61. New York: Garland.

Franklin, Benjamin, 1923, *The Autobiography of Benjamin Franklin*. Reprint. n.p.: Houghton Mifflin.

Garrett, Duane, 1995, *Angels and the New Spirituality*. Nashville: Broadman & Holman.

Garrett, Susan, 1989, *The Demise of the Devil: Magic and the Demonic in Luke's Writings*. Minneapolis: Fortress.

Geertz, Clifford, 1960, *The Religion of Java*. New York: Free Press.

Goldingay, John, 1989, *Daniel*. WBC. Dallas: Word.

Green, Michael, 1987, *2 Peter and Jude*. TNTC. Leicester: IVP.

Greenlee, David, 1994, Territorial Spirits Reconsidered. *Missiology* 22: 507-14.

Guelich, R. A., 1991, Spiritual Warfare: Jesus, Paul and Peretti. *Pneuma: Journal of Pentecostal Studies* 13: 33-64.

Guinness, Os, 1983, *The Gravedigger File: Papers on the Subversion of the Modern Church*. London: Hodder & Stoughton.

Guinness, Os, 1992, Sounding Out the Idols of Church Growth. In *No God But God: Breaking with the Idols of our Age*. Os Guinness and John Steel, eds. Chicago: Moody.

Guinness, Os, 1993, *Dining with the Devil: The Megachurch Movement Flirts with Modernity*. Grand Rapids: Baker.

Guinness, Os, 1994, *Fit Bodies, Fat Minds: Why Evangelicals Don't Think and What to Do About It*. Grand Rapids: Baker.

Hagin, Kenneth, 1993, *The Triumphant Church: Dominion Over All the Powers of Darkness*. Tulsa, OK: Faith Library.

Hefner, Robert, 1993, Of Faith and Commitment: Christian Conversion in Muslim Java. In *Conversion to Christianity: Historical and Anthropo-*

logical Perspectives on a Great Transformation. Robert Hefner, ed. Pp. 99-125. Berkeley: University of California Press.

Hengel, Martin, 1989, *The Zealots*. Edinburgh: T&T Clark.

Hesselgrave, David, 1978, What Causes Religious Movements to Grow? In *Dynamic Religious Movements: Case Studies of Rapidly Growing Religious Movements Around the World*. David Hesselgrave, ed. Pp 297-326. Grand Rapids: Baker.

Hesselgrave, David, 1994, *Scripture and Strategy: The Use of the Bible in Post-modern Church and Mission*. Pasadena: William Carey.

Hiebert, Paul, 1993, The Evangelical Expansion South of the American Border. In *Secularization, Rationalism and Sectarianism: Essays in Honour of Bryan Wilson*. Eileen Barker, James Beckford, Karel Dobbelacre, eds. Pp. 101-24. Oxford: Clarendon Press.

Hiebert, Paul, 1982, The Flaw of the Excluded Middle. *Missiology* 10: 35-47.

Hiebert, Paul, 1989, Healing and the Kingdom. In *Wonders and the World*. James Coggins & Paul Hiebert, eds. Pp 109-52. Hillsboro, KS: Kindred Press.

Hiebert, Paul, 1994, *Anthropological Reflections on Missiological Issues*. Grand Rapids: Baker.

Hiebert, Theodore, 1992, Warrior, Divine. In *Anchor Bible Dictionary*. David Freedman, ed. 6:876-880. Garden City, NY: Doubleday.

Horowitz, Irving, 1994, Critical Responses to Friendly Critics. In *The Democratic Imagination*. Ray Rist, ed. Pp. 499-599. New Brunswick, NJ: Transaction.

Hull, Bill, 1992, Is the Church Growth Movement Really Working? In *Power Religion*. Michael Horton, ed. Pp. 139-59. Chicago: Moody.

Hunt, Robert, Lee Kam Hing and John Roxborogh, 1992, *Christianity in Malaysia: A Denominational History*. Petaling Jaya, Malaysia: Pelanduk.

Hunter, James, 1983, *American Evangelicalism and the Quandary of Modernity*. New Brunswick, NJ: Rutgers University Press.

Jacobs, Cindy, 1993, Dealing with Strongholds. In *Breaking Strongholds in Your City: How to Use Spiritual Mapping to Make Your Prayers More Strategic, Effective and Targeted*. C. Peter Wagner, ed. Pp. 73-95. Ventura, CA: Regal.

Johnstone, Ronald, 1992, *Religion in Society: A Sociology of Religion*. Englewood Cliffs, NJ: Prentice Hall.

Keil, C. F., 1985, *Biblical Commentary on the Book of Daniel*. Grand Rapids: Eerdmans.

Kelly, J. N. D., 1969, *A Commentary on the Epistles of Peter and of Jude.* BNTC. London: Black.

Kerr, Hugh, 1943, *A Compend of Luther's Theology.* Philadelphia: Westminster.

Keyes, Charles, 1993, Why the Thai Are Not Christians: Buddhist and Christian Conversion in Thailand. In *Conversion to Christianity: Historical and Anthropological Perspectives on a Great Transformation.* Robert Hefner, ed. Pp. 259-83. Berkeley: University of California Press.

Koentjaraningrat, 1989, *Javanese Culture.* Oxford: Oxford University.

Kopfermann, Wolfgang, 1994, *Macht ohne Auftrag: Warum ich mich nicht an der „geistlichen Kriegführung" beteilige.* Emmelsbuell, Germany: C&P.

Kraft, Charles, 1989, *Christianity with Power: Your Worldview and Your Experience of the Supernatural.* Ann Arbor: Servant.

Ladd, George E., 1972, *A Commentary on the Revelation of John.* Grand Rapids: Eerdmans.

Lawson, Steven, 1991, Defeating Territorial Spirits. In *Engaging the Enemy: How to Fight and Defeat Territorial Spirits.* C. Peter Wagner, ed. Pp. 29-41. Ventura, CA: Regal.

Lea, Larry, 1991, Binding the Strongman. In *Engaging the Enemy: How to Fight and Defeat Territorial Spirits.* C. Peter Wagner, ed. Pp. 83-95. Ventura, CA: Regal.

Lincoln, Andrew, 1990, *Ephesians.* WBC. Dallas: Word.

Loewen, Jacob, 1986, Which God Do Missionaries Preach? *Missiology* 14: 3-19.

Lorenzo, Victor, 1993, Evangelizing a City Dedicated to Darkness. In *Breaking Strongholds in Your City: How to Use Spiritual Mapping to Make Your Prayers More Strategic, Effective and Targeted.* C. Peter Wagner, ed. Pp. 171-193. Ventura, CA: Regal.

Louth, Andrew 1989, *Denys the Areopagite.* London: Geoffrey Chapman.

MacGregor, Geddes, 1988, *Angels: Ministers of Grace.* New York: Paragon House.

MacMullen, Ramsay, 1984, *Christianizing the Roman Empire (AD 100-400).* New Haven: Yale University Press.

Martin, David, 1990, *Tongues of Fire: The Explosion of Protestantism in Latin America.* Oxford: Blackwell.

Mathews, R. Arthur, 1972, *Born for Battle: 31 Studies on Spiritual Warfare.* London: OMF.

McConnell, D. R., 1988, *A Different Gospel: A Historical and Biblical Analysis of the Modern Faith Movement.* Peabody, MA: Hendrickson.

McGregor, Mark and Bev Klopp, 1993, Mapping and Discerning Seattle, Washington. In *Breaking Strongholds in Your City*. C. Peter Wagner, ed. Pp. 197-222. Ventura, CA: Regal.

McKinney, Carol, 1994, Conversion to Christianity: A Bajju Case Study. *Missiology* 22:147-65.

Meyers, Carol and Eric Meyers, 1987, *Haggai, Zechariah 1-8*. ABC. Garden City, NY: Doubleday.

Morris, Leon, 1987, *The Book of Revelation*. TNTC. Leicester: IVP.

Mounce, Robert, 1977, *The Book of Revelation*. NICNT. Grand Rapids: Eerdmans.

Murphy, Ed, 1992, *The Handbook for Spiritual Warfare*. Nashville: Nelson.

Newsom, Carol, 1992, Angels. In *Anchor Bible Dictionary*. David Freedman, ed. 1:248-53. Garden City, NY: Doubleday.

Nickelsburg, George, 1981, *Jewish Literature Between the Bible and the Mishnah*. London: SCM.

Nida, Eugene, 1974, *Understanding Latin Americans: With Specific Reference to Religious Values and Meanings*. Pasadena: William Carey Library.

Noonan, Laurence, 1965, The First Jesuit Mission in Malacca: A Study of the Use of the Portuguese Trading Centre as a Base for Christian Missionary Expansion During the Years 1545 to 1552. Unpub MA thesis. Perth, Australia: University of Western Australia.

Oepke, Albrecht and Karl Kuhn, 1967, *Panoplia*. In *Theological Dictionary of the New Testament*. Gerhard Kittel and Gerhard Friedrick, eds. 5:295-302. Grand Rapids: Eerdmans.

Oswalt, John, 1986, *The Book of Isaiah: Chapters 1-39*. Grand Rapids: Eerdmans.

Otis, George, Jr., 1991, *The Last of the Giants*. Tarrytown, NY: Chosen.

Otis, George, Jr., 1993, An Overview of Spiritual Mapping. In *Engaging the Enemy: How to Fight and Defeat Territorial Spirits*. C. Peter Wagner, ed. Pp. 29-47. Ventura, CA: Regal.

Page, Sydney, 1995, *Powers of Evil: A Biblical Study of Satan and Demons*. Grand Rapids: Baker.

Pawson, David, 1992, *The Fourth Wave: Charismatics and Evangelicals, Are We Ready to Come Together?* London: Hodder & Stoughton.

Peretti, Frank, 1986, *This Present Darkness*. Westchester, IL: Crossway.

Peretti, Frank, 1989, *Piercing the Darkness*. Westchester, IL: Crossway.

Peskett, Howard, 1996, God's Missionary Railway According to Stott and Wagner. *EMQ* 32: 480-84.

Postman, Neil, 1993, *Technopoly: The Surrender of Culture to Technology*. New York: Vintage.

Powlison, David, 1995, *Power Encounters: Reclaiming Spiritual Warfare*. Grand Rapids: Baker.

Priest, Robert, Thomas Campbell, and Bradford Mullen, 1995, Missiological Syncretism: The New Animistic Paradigm. In *Spiritual Power and Missions: Raising the Issues*. Edward Rommen, ed. Pp. 9-87. Pasadena: William Carey.

Ranger, Terence, 1993, The Local and the Global in Southern African Religious History. In *Conversion to Christianity: Historical and Anthropological Perspectives on a Great Transformation*. Robert Hefner, ed. Pp. 65-98. Berkeley: University of California Press.

Read, William, 1965, *New Patterns of Church Growth in Brazil*. Grand Rapids: Eerdmans.

Read, William, Victor Monterroso and Harmon Johnson, 1969, *Latin American Church Growth*. Grand Rapids: Eerdmans.

Reddin, Opal, 1989, Power for Spiritual Warfare. In *Power Encounter: A Pentecostal Perspective: Can a Christian Be Inhabited by Demons?* Opal Reddin, ed. Pp. 187-214. Springfield, MO: Central Bible College Press.

Redfield, Robert, 1941, *The Folk Culture of Yucatan*. Chicago: University of Chicago.

Redfield, Robert, 1956, *Peasant Society and Culture: An Anthropological Approach to Civilization*. Chicago: University of Chicago.

Reid, Daniel, 1993, Triumph. In *Dictionary of Paul and his Letters*. G. Hawthorne, R. Martin, D. Reid, eds. Pp. 946-54. Downers Grove, IL: IVP.

Robb, John, 1993, Satan's Tactics in Building and Maintaining His Kingdom of Darkness. *International Journal of Frontier Missions* 10:173-84.

Rogers, Everett, 1983, *Diffusion of Innovations*. New York: Free Press.

Russell, D. S., 1964, *The Method and Message of Jewish Apocalyptic 200 BC–AD 10*. Philadelphia: Westminster.

Russell, D. S., 1989, *Daniel: An Active Volcano*. Louisville: Westminster/ John Knox.

Russell, Jeffrey, 1977, *The Devil: Perceptions of Evil from Antiquity to Primitive Christianity*. Ithaca, NY: Cornell University Press.

Russell, Jeffrey, 1981, *Satan: The Early Christian Tradition*. Ithaca, NY: Cornell University Press.

Russell, Jeffrey, 1984, *Lucifer: The Devil in the Middle Ages*. Ithaca, NY: Cornell University Press.

Schurhammer, Georg, 1980, *Francis Xavier. His Life, His Times. Vol 3: Indonesia, 1545-1549*. Rome: Jesuit Historical Institute.

Schurhammer, Georg, 1982, *Francis Xavier. His Life, His Times. Vol 4: Japan and China, 1549-1553*. Rome: Jesuit Historical Institute.

Schürer, Emil, 1979, *The History of the Jewish People in the Age of Jesus Christ (175 BC–AD 135)*. G. Vermes, F. Millar & M. Black, eds. Vol 2. Edinburgh: T&T Clark.

Silvoso, Edgardo, 1991, Prayer Power in Argentina. In *Engaging the Enemy: How to Fight and Defeat Territorial Spirits*. C. Peter Wagner, ed. Pp. 109-115. Ventura, CA: Regal.

Sjöberg, Kjell, 1993, Spiritual Mapping for Prophetic Prayer Actions. In *Breaking Strongholds in Your City*. C. Peter Wagner, ed. Pp. 97-119. Ventura, CA: Regal.

Spiro, Melford, 1967, *Burmese Supernaturalism: A Study in the Explanation and Reduction of Suffering*. Englewood Cliffs, NJ: Prentice-Hall.

Sterk, Vernon, 1991, Territorial Spirits and Evangelization in Hostile Environments. In *Engaging the Enemy: How to Fight and Defeat Territorial Spirits*. C. Peter Wagner, ed. Pp. 145-163. Ventura, CA: Regal.

Steward, Edith, 1917, *The Life of St. Francis Xavier: Evangelist, Explorer, Mystic*. Kingsway, W.C.: Headley Bros.

Studer, Basilio, 1992, Demon. In *Encyclopedia of the Early Church*. A. D. Berardino, ed. 1.226-27. Cambridge: James Clarke.

Surburg, Raymond, 1975, *Introduction to the Intertestamental Period*. St Louis: Concordia.

Taylor, Geraldine, 1944, *Behind the Ranges*. London: Lutterworth.

Taylor, Mike, 1993, *Do Demons Rule Your Town? An Examination of the 'Territorial Spirits' Theory*. London: Grace.

Teixeira, Manuel, 1961, *The Portuguese Missions in Malacca and Singapore (1511-1958). Vol 1: Malacca*. Lisboa: Agencia Geral Do Ultramar.

Thomas, Keith, 1973, *Religion and the Decline of Magic: Studies in Popular Beliefs in Sixteenth- and Seventeenth-Century England*. Harmondsworth: Penguin.

Thompson, Laurence, 1979, *Chinese Religion: An Introduction*. Belmont, CA: Wadsworth.

van Rheenen, Gailyn, 1991, *Communicating Christ in Animistic Contexts*. Grand Rapids: Baker.

Veith, Gene, 1994, *A Guide to Contemporary Culture*. Leicester: Crossway.

Vogt, Evon, 1970, *The Zinacantecos of Mexico: A Modern Maya Way of Life*. New York: Holt, Rinehart and Winston.

Wagner, C. Peter, 1973a, *Look Out! The Pentecostals Are Coming*. Carol Stream: Creation.

Wagner, C. Peter, 1973b, Pragmatic Strategy for Tomorrow's Mission. In *God, Man and Church Growth*. A. R. Tippet, ed. Grand Rapids: Eerdmans.

Wagner, C. Peter, 1984a, *Leading Your Church to Growth*. Ventura, CA: Regal.

Wagner, C. Peter, 1984b, *Your Church Can Grow: Seven Vital Signs of a Healthy Church*. Ventura, CA: Regal.

Wagner, C. Peter, 1986, *Spiritual Power and Church Growth*. London: Hodder & Stoughton.

Wagner, C. Peter, 1987, *Strategies for Church Growth: Tools for Effective Mission and Evangelism*. Ventura, CA: Regal.

Wagner, C. Peter, 1988a, *How to Have a Healing Ministry Without Making Your Church Sick*. Eastbourne: Monarch.

Wagner, C. Peter, 1988b, *The Third Wave of the Holy Spirit: Encountering the Power of Signs and Wonders*. Ann Arbor: Vine.

Wagner, C. Peter, 1990, Territorial Spirits. In *Wrestling with Dark Angels: Toward a Deeper Understanding of the Supernatural Force in Spiritual Warfare*. C. Peter Wagner and F. Douglas Pennoyer, eds. Pp. 73-91. Ventura, CA: Regal.

Wagner, C. Peter, 1991a, Spiritual Warfare. In *Engaging the Enemy: How to Fight and Defeat Territorial Spirits*. C. Peter Wagner, ed. Pp. 3-27. Ventura, CA: Regal.

Wagner, C. Peter, 1991b, Territorial Spirits. In *Engaging the Enemy: How to Fight and Defeat Territorial Spirits*. C. Peter Wagner, ed. Pp. 43-50. Ventura, CA: Regal.

Wagner, C. Peter, 1992, *Warfare Prayer: How to Seek God's Power and Protection in the Battle To Build His Kingdom*. Ventura, CA: Regal.

Wagner, C. Peter, 1993a, Introduction. In *Breaking Strongholds in Your City: How to Use Spiritual Mapping to Make Your Prayers More Strategic, Effective and Targeted*. C. Peter Wagner, ed. Pp. 11-26. Ventura, CA: Regal.

Wagner, C. Peter, 1993b, The Visible and the Invisible. In *Breaking Strongholds in Your City: How to Use Spiritual Mapping to Make Your Prayers More Strategic, Effective and Targeted*. C. Peter Wagner, ed. Pp. 49-72. Ventura, CA: Regal.

Wagner, C. Peter, 1993c, Summary: Mapping Your Community. In *Breaking Strongholds in Your City: How to Use Spiritual Mapping to Make Your Prayers More Strategic, Effective and Targeted*. C. Peter Wagner, ed. Pp. 223-232. Ventura, CA: Regal.

Wagner, C. Peter, 1993d, *Churches That Pray: How Prayer Can Revitalize Your Congregation and Break Down the Walls Between Your Church and Your Community*. Ventura, CA: Regal.

Wagner, C. Peter, 1994, *Spreading the Fire: A New Look at Acts. Book 1: Acts 1-8*. Ventura, CA: Regal.

Wagner, C. Peter, 1995a, *Lighting the World: A New Look at Acts. Book 2: Acts 9-15*. Ventura, CA: Regal.

Wagner, C. Peter, 1995b, *Blazing the Way: A New Look at Acts. Book 3: Acts 16-28*. Ventura, CA: Regal.

Wagner, C. Peter, 1996, *Confronting the Powers: How the New Testament Church Experienced the Power of Strategic-Level Spiritual Warfare*. Ventura, CA: Regal.

Wagner, C. Peter, 1997, *Praying with Power: How to Pray Effectively and Hear Clearly from God*. Ventura, CA: Regal.

Wagner, C. Peter, ed., 1991, *Engaging the Enemy: How to Fight and Defeat Territorial Spirits*. Ventura, CA: Regal.

Wagner, C. Peter, ed., 1993, *Breaking Strongholds in Your City: How to Use Spiritual Mapping to Make Your Prayers More Strategic, Effective and Targeted*. Ventura, CA: Regal.

Wagner, C. Peter and F. Douglas Pennoyer, eds., 1990, *Wrestling with Dark Angels: Toward a Deeper Understanding of the Supernatural Forces in Spiritual Warfare*. Ventura, CA: Regal.

Wall, Robert, 1991, *Revelation*. NIBC. Peabody, MA: Hendrickson.

Warner, Timothy, 1986, Power Encounter with the Demonic. In *Evangelism on the Cutting Edge*. Robert Coleman, ed. Pp. 89-101. Old Tappan, NJ: Fleming Revell.

Warner, Timothy, 1991a, Dealing with Territorial Demons. In *Engaging the Enemy*. C. Peter Wagner, ed. Pp. 51-54. Ventura, CA: Regal.

Warner, Timothy, 1991b, *Spiritual Warfare*. Wheaton, IL: Crossway.

Watson, Duane, 1988, *Invention, Arrangement and Style: Rhetorical Criticism of Jude and 2 Peter*. Atlanta: Scholars.

Watts, John, 1985, *Isaiah 1-33*. WBC. Waco, TX: Word.

Weber, Max, 1991, The Social Psychology of the World Religions. In *From Max Weber: Essays in Sociology*. H. H. Garth and C. W. Mills eds. London: Routledge. [original publication 1923]

Wee, Vivienne, 1977, Religion and Ritual Among the Chinese of Singapore: An Ethnographic Study. Unpub M.Soc.Sci. thesis. Singapore: National University of Singapore.

Weyer, Johann, 1991, *Witches, Devils, and Doctors in the Renaissance.* Binghamton, NY: State University of New York. [original publication 1563]

White, Thomas, 1991, Understanding Principalities and Powers. In *Engaging the Enemy.* C. Peter Wagner, ed. Pp. 59-67. Ventura, CA: Regal.

Whiteman, Darrell, 1983, *Melanesians and Missionaries: An Ethnohistorical Study of Social and Religious Change in the Southwest Pacific.* Pasadena: William Carey Library

Willis, Avery Jr., 1977, *Indonesian Revival: Why Two Million Came to Christ.* Pasadena: William Carey Library.

Wilson, J. M., 1979, Angel. *International Standard Bible Encyclopedia.* Geoffrey Bromiley, ed. 1:124-27. Grand Rapids: Eerdmans.

Wimber, John with Kevin Springer, 1990, *The Dynamics of Spiritual Growth.* London: Hodder & Stoughton.

Wink, Walter, 1984, *Naming the Powers: The Language of Power in the New Testament.* Philadelphia: Fortress.

Wright, N. T., 1986, *The Epistles of Paul to the Colossians and to Philemon: An Introduction and Commentary.* TNTC, Leicester: IVP.

Yamauchi, Edwin, 1980, *New Testament Cities in Western Asia Minor.* Grand Rapids: Baker.

INDEX OF NAMES

BIBLE REFERENCES

Chuck Lowe studied at Oral Roberts University (B.A.); Westminster Theological Seminary (M.A.R.); and the Australian College of Theology (Th.D. under Leon Morris). He has served with OMF at Singapore Bible College since 1984, where he teaches New Testament interpretation, theology and preaching. He is also theological researcher with OMF since 1995. His research interests are in Chinese folk religion and sociology of religion. Chuck is married to Irene Wong, a Malaysian Chinese, and they have two children.